Conversations with James Thurber

Literary Conversations Series

Peggy Whitman Prenshaw
General Editor

Tibor Hirsch

Conversations
with James Thurber

Edited by
Thomas Fensch

University Press of Mississippi
Jackson and London

Library of Congress Cataloging-in-Publication Data

Thurber, James, 1894-1961.
    Conversations with James Thurber / edited by Thomas Fensch.
        p.   cm. — (Literary conversations series)
    Includes index.
    ISBN 0-87805-409-X (alk. paper). — ISBN 0-87805-410-3 (pbk. :
alk. paper)
        1. Thurber, James, 1894-1961—Interviews.   2. Authors,
American—20th century—Interviews.   3. Humorists, American—20th
century—Interviews.   I. Fensch, Thomas.   II. Title.   III. Series.
    PS3539.H94Z464   1989   89-32215
    818'.5209—dc20   CIP

British Library Cataloguing-in-Publication data is available.

Books by James Thurber

Is Sex Necessary? or Why You Feel the Way You Do (With E. B. White). New York: Harper & Brothers, 1929.

The Owl in the Attic and Other Perplexities. New York: Harper & Brothers, 1931.

The Seal in the Bedroom and Other Predicaments. New York: Harper & Brothers, 1932.

My Life and Hard Times. New York: Harper & Brothers, 1933.

The Middle-Aged Man on the Flying Trapeze. New York: Harper & Brothers, 1935.

Let Your Mind Alone! and Other More or Less Inspirational Pieces. New York: Harper & Brothers, 1937.

The Last Flower, A Parable in Pictures. New York: Harper & Brothers, 1939.

Fables for Our Times and Famous Poems Illustrated. New York: Harper & Brothers, 1940.

The Male Animal (With Elliott Nugent). New York: Random House, 1940.

My World—And Welcome to It. New York: Harcourt, Brace and Company, 1942.

Many Moons. New York: Harcourt, Brace and Company, 1943.

Men, Women and Dogs. New York: Harcourt, Brace and Company, 1943.

The Great Quillow. New York: Harcourt, Brace and Company, 1944.

The Thurber Carnival. New York: Harper & Brothers, 1945.

The White Deer. New York: Harcourt, Brace and Company, 1945.

The Beast in Me and Other Animals. New York: Harcourt, Brace and Company, 1948.

The 13 Clocks. New York: Simon and Schuster, 1950.

The Thurber Album. New York: Simon and Schuster, 1952.

Thurber Country. New York: Simon and Schuster, 1953.

Thurber's Dogs. New York: Simon and Schuster, 1955.

Further Fables for Our Time. New York: Simon and Schuster, 1956.

Alarms and Diversions. New York: Harper & Brothers, 1957.

The Wonderful O. New York: Simon and Schuster, 1957.

The Years with Ross. Boston: Atlantic, Little, Brown and Company, 1959.

Lanterns and Lances. New York: Harper & Brothers, 1961.

Credos and Curios. New York: Harper & Row, Inc., 1962.

A Thurber Carnival. New York: Samuel French, Inc., 1962.

Thurber and Company. New York: Harper & Row, 1966.

Contents

Introduction

"Comedy is his chosen field," Malcolm Cowley wrote of James Thurber, but while Thurber's range of effects is deliberately limited, within that range nobody writes better than he does, that is, more clearly and flexibly, with a deeper feeling for the genius of language and the value of words. Cowley, in his essay "Lions and Lemmings, Toads and Tigers" in *Thurber: A Collection of Critical Essays,* continued, "He prefers the familiar words that would be used in conversation without a self-conscious pause. His art consists in arranging them so that they give the impression of standing cleanly and separately on the page, each in its place like stones in a well-built wall."

Thurber, who may well stand unchallenged as America's twentieth-century Mark Twain—in 1958 he became the first American since Twain to be invited to join the editors of *Punch* during their weekly luncheon—established himself as a writer and cartoonist after joining the *New Yorker* staff in 1927. Charles S. Holmes wrote, in *The Clocks of Columbus: The Literary Career of James Thurber,* his "creative talent flowered in the years after he joined the magazine." *Is Sex Necessary?* (1929), *The Owl in the Attic* (1931), *The Seal in the Bedroom* (1932), *My Life and Hard Times* (1933), and *The Middle-Aged Man on the Flying Trapeze* (1935) established him as a writer and cartoonist of rare originality. Here were the subjects, characters, and themes which identified his work up to the period of his blindness: the domestic scene and the trivia which somehow explode into major conflicts; the timid day-dreamy men and the aggressive practical women; the view of marriage as a state of undeclared war; the celebration of the natural, the individual, the eccentric as against conventions, formulas, and systems of all kinds; and above all, the constant and surprising interplay of reality and fantasy."

In the Prospectus for the first issue of the *New Yorker,* founder and editor Harold Ross promised that his new magazine would be a model of sophistication—it would not, he declared, be written and edited for "the little old lady in Dubuque." Then, however, James Thurber joined the staff as Managing Editor, quickly working his way *downward* to staff writer, hailing from Columbus, Ohio. Literally only hundreds of miles apart, Thurber's Columbus and Ross's Dubuque were figuratively identical. Thurber joined Ross, the relatively unschooled journalist from the Rocky Mountains, E. B. White, and others to craft the *New Yorker* into the sophisticated magazine Ross envisioned. No wonder they seemed surprised that it succeeded.

Thurber had moved from his provincial hometown to the urbane world of the *New Yorker,* but his idyllic world of Columbus never left him. "I am never very far away from Ohio in my thoughts and . . . the clocks that strike in my dreams are always the clocks of Columbus," Thurber acknowledged in an oft-quoted line from his speech/ essay "Thurber on Humor," given when the Ohioana Library Association awarded him the Sesquicentennial Medal in 1953. Thurber returned to Ohio again and again for inspiration and to mine material, especially for *The Thurber Album* (1952), the wry portrait of his real (and mythical) family life in Columbus.

"Confusion, chaos, eccentricity—these are the qualities Thurber discovers and delights in as he looks back at the world of his boyhood." Holmes, cited above, wrote in "Reality Twisted to the Right: *My Life and Hard Times*" in *Thurber: A Collection of Critical Essays,* "and in telling the story of those early days he consistently reshapes reality, stylizes and fictionalizes it, to bring it closer to the world of fantasy. Long before he put any of it down on paper, he was thinking about it, working it over in his memory and imagination, shaping it into anecdotes for the entertainment of his friends at parties . . . . By the time he came to write it all down, fact and fantasy had become so perfectly assimilated to one another that there was no longer any noticeable difference between them."

Thurber was well-served by the years of working material over "in his memory and imagination" when increasing blindness, beginning about 1940, forced him to compose everything mentally, revising and editing it, then dictating to a secretary. Thurber, like other writers— except for his claim to a near photographic memory—revised and edited his own memories as well and, presented them in slightly different forms in various interviews.

And what of those interviews? No doubt, if we were to interview

Thurber today, he would talk more about the things he always talked about:

• Anecdotes and family members from his life in Columbus, of course, perhaps slight variations on the material included in *The Thurber Album* or *My Life and Hard Times;*

• His days as a student at Ohio State University: struggles with botany classes and his inability to see through a microscope; ROTC classes; football players he knew and games he saw; conflicts about academic freedom he witnessed (which later appeared in his play *The Male Animal*); his work for the Ohio State University newspaper and humor magazine; the professors he knew; the musicals he wrote which were produced on campus;

• His days in Europe as a code clerk and newspaperman, when he had to recreate entire stories from a few words of coded copy from the newspaper wire services;

• His early days in New York City, when he joined the staff of the *New Yorker.* His astonished discovery that he had been appointed Managing Editor without his knowledge and his rapid demotion to staff writer. Comparisons of the early days of the *New Yorker* to later days, when he had resigned from the staff to free-lance. Anecdotes of various *New Yorker* staff writers, from early to later years;

• The origins of his drawings and the art (or lack of it) in his technique;

• Word games and mental puzzles that fascinated him;

• His blindness—its origins and subsequent affect on his work— and related to his blindness, his techniques for writing and editing mentally, and then dictating material for publication. How his blindness changed his perceptions of the world;

• His imagination and memory in all their various aspects;

• The Thurber Men he created, the Thurber Women, the constant and shifting Battle of the Sexes and the general Superiority of Women (His 1953 Associated Press Interview "Says Superwomen Will Force Peace" sounds refreshingly current);

• Thurber dogs in particular and animals in general;

• The growing decline of theater in America;

• Humor—what it is—and how to write it;

And various combinations of anecdotes, complaints and opinions about the world.

The interview is a format that Thurber found friendly. In *The Clocks of Columbus: The Literary Career of James Thurber,* Charles Holmes wrote that Thurber "seldom refused a request (for an interview), partly because he was an old newspaperman and sympathized with reporters, and partly because he was one of the great talkers of his time. He had opinions on everything and liked to express them; he was a superb story-teller and mimic, and he loved an audience. Over the years, he made the interview-monologue into an art form, the oral equivalent of the autobiographical essay which he had developed to perfection in his prose. It was, perhaps, the form most congenial to him as he grew older. The key to it was the balance between the casual, conventional manner—its spontaneous quality— and the basic structure of ready-made topics, anecdotes and routines which gave it substance and coherence. Depending upon how the particular interview was going, Thurber would rely mostly on his standard anecdotes or introduce fresh material and improvise on it as the spirit moved him."

At least one, however, of the many who interviewed Thurber had harsh criticism rather than praise for him in his later days. A young John Updike complained about Thurber in an article, "Writers I have Met," published in the August 11, 1968 issue of *The New York Times Book Review.* Updike described Thurber as "a big-boned blind giant . . . and there could have been no way of anticipating the alarming way his eyes caromed around the refracting magnification of his glasses." Updike criticized not only Thurber's blindness but his memory, writing, "Though Thurber cocked his head alertly at my poor fawning attempts to make conversation, these attempts did not appreciably distract him from the anecdotes of Columbus, Ohio, he had told a thousand times before, and that I had read 10 years before in their definitive, printed version. Pages of *The Thurber Album* and *My Life and Hard Times* issued from his lips virtually intact."

With his friendlier mien, Holmes continued in *The Clocks of Columbus* to describe Thurber's interview talents as a kind of autobiography. "Some interviews, like those conducted by Plimpton and Steele or Alistair Cooke,* were carefully structured, wide-ranging

---

*"James Thurber: In Conversation with Alistair Cooke" *The Atlantic Monthly,* Aug. 1956. Because of copyright restrictions, that article was not available for this volume.

discussions of Thurber's aims, habits and tastes as an artist. In those conversations Thurber is the artist as autobiographer, talking seriously and entertainingly about how he got started, about the people who influenced him, about the craft of writing and his personal work habits, about his drawings, and about the fate of humor in the modern world." Most of the interviews with Thurber were less formal and more spontaneous performances, of course, and in these he jumped chattily among the subjects which formed his standard repertory, almost always adding something not told before. Holmes admitted, "Thurber was interviewed so often that he repeated himself without compunction, falling back on ideas and anecdotes which he had already used in other interviews or, even worse, already committed to print."

Consider, however, that as Thurber's fame as a writer and artist grew and grew, his eyesight faded and faded. In the early 1940s, he was universally famous and and acclaimed, and simultaneously he was almost totally blind. He could write only by mental composition. He was totally unable to draw. Left with his imagination and his near photographic memory, to tell and retell anecdotes from his sighted past was valuable currency indeed.

Of Thurber's later interviews, Holmes wrote in *Clocks of Columbus,* "In the late 1950s the interviews, like his writing, become less personal and anecdotal and more didactic and critical." And in his biography, *Thurber,* Burton Bernstein claimed that Thurber in his last days became unruly, sullen and mean-spirited, throwing glasses at cocktail parties and creating scenes. After a career in which he reached the pinnacle of American letters, after he created the Thurber world with all its amiable and slightly askew humor, after a life in which he tolerated and even joked about his blindness, who could blame him for finally railing against it?

In these pages you can hear Thurber again, visualize the Thurber men, the Thurber women and the dogs and the drawings, which Dorothy Parker once described in her Introduction to *The Seal in the Bedroom and Other Predicaments* as having "the outer semblance of unbaked cookies." Thurber's characters have, she added: "A touching quality. They expected so little of life; they remember the old discouragements and await the new. They are not shrewd people, nor even bright and we must be very patient with them. Lambs in the world of wolves, they are, and there is on them a protracted innocence."

Bernstein's biography concludes with a fitting summary of Thurber's life and work: "What he did was manufacture a unique world with its own creatures, its own mores, its own energy, its own foibles, its own madness—all remarkably similar to the real world, similar enough so we can laugh and then perhaps feel vaguely uncomfortable. It is a creation not to be taken lightly.

"As for the man, he passed through with brillance, cheered the population, suffered and caused some suffering, and then passed on. But most of all, he left something elegant and important behind."

Interviews in this collection have not been edited since their original, except to correct obvious typesetting errors. Headlines may have been changed slightly to reflect the style in this series. Duplication questions in separate articles have been retained to show similarities or differences over time.

This book is for Dr. Tetsumaro "Ted" Hayashi, with admiration and respect.

Bibliography

Bernstein, Burton. *Thurber.* New York: Dodd, Mead and Co., 1975.

Holmes, Charles S. *The Clocks of Columbus: The Literary Career of James Thurber.* New York: Atheneum Publishers, Inc., 1972.

Holmes, Charles S., editor. *Thurber: A Collection of Critical Essays.* Englewood Cliffs, NJ: Prentice-Hall, Inc., 1974.

Morseberger, Robert E. *James Thurber.* New York: Twayne Publishers, Inc., 1974.

Chronology

1894   James Grover Thurber is born in Columbus, Ohio, 8 December, the son of Charles L. and Mary Fisher Thurber.

1901   Thurber is blinded in his left eye when his older brother William shot him with an arrow, while the family is temporarily living in Washington, D.C.

1903   Family returns to Columbus.

1913   Thurber enters Ohio State University.

1916   He meets Elliott Nugent and begins participating in O.S.U. campus activities.

1917   Writes for the Ohio State University newspaper *The Ohio State Lantern* and the humor magazine, *The Sun Dial*

1918   Thurber is named editor of *The Sun Dial.* He leaves Ohio State in June without a degree and becomes a code clerk for the State Department, in Washington, D.C., then in Paris.

1918–20   Works in Paris

1920   Returns to Columbus and becomes a reporter for *The Columbus Dispatch*

1921   Writes and directs musicals for Ohio State University's Scarlet Mask Club

1922   Marries Althea Adams

1923   Writes Sunday column "Credos and Curios" for *The Columbus Dispatch*

1924   Leaves *The Columbus Dispatch* to become a free-lance writer; writes for *The Christian Science Monitor* and *The Wheeling Intelligencer*

1925   Returns to France and begins a novel, subsequently unfinished. Works for the Paris editor of *The Chicago Tribune* and later, the Rivera edition.

1926   Returns to the U.S. Begins working for *The New York Evening Post* as a reporter.

1927   Meets E. B. White and Harold Ross and is hired by *The New Yorker*

1929   His first book, *Is Sex Necessary?*, co-authored with E. B. White, is published by Harper & Brothers.

1931   *The New Yorker* begins publishing his drawings. His daughter Rosemary is born 7 October. His second book, *The Owl in the Attic and Other Perplexities* is published by Harper & Brothers.

1932   *The Seal in the Bedroom and Other Predicaments* is published by Harper & Brothers.

1933   *My Life and Hard Times* is published by Harper & Brothers.

1934   Has a one-man show of his drawings, New York

1935   *The Middle Aged Man on the Flying Trapeze* is published by Harper & Brothers. Thurber is divorced from Althea Adams; he marries Helen Wismer. He begins free-lancing.

1937   *Let Your Mind Alone! and Other More or Less Inspira-tional Pieces* is published by Harper & Brothers. Has shows of his drawings in Hollywood and London.

1937–38   Travels in France

1939   *The Last Flower, A Parable in Pictures* is published by Harper & Brothers. His most famous short story, "The Secret Life of Walter Mitty" is published in *The New Yorker.* Collaborates with Elliott Nugent on *The Male Animal.*

1940   *Fables for Our Time and Famous Poems Illustrated* is published by Harper & Brothers. *The Male Animal* is produced.

1940–41   Thurber has a series of eye operations.

1942   *My World — And Welcome to It* is published by Harcourt, Brace and Company. *The Male Animal* is produced as a film.

1943   *Men, Women and Dogs, a Book of Drawings* is published by Harcourt, Brace and Company. *Many Moons* is published, also by Harcourt, Brace.

1944   *The Great Quillow* is published by Harcourt, Brace and Company.

1945   *The Thurber Carnival* and *The White Deer* are published, by Harper & Brothers and Harcourt, Brace and Company, respectively.

1947   *The Secret Life of Walter Mitty* is filmed; produced by Samuel Goldwyn, with Danny Kaye as Mitty. Thurber calls the film "The Public Life of Danny Kaye" and apologizes for it before release.

1948   *The Beast in Me and Other Animals* is published by
            Harcourt, Brace and Company.

1950   *The Thirteen Clocks* is published by Simon & Schuster.
            Thurber receives an honorary doctorate from Kenyon
            College, Ohio.

1951   Receives honorary doctorate from Williams College,
            Massachusetts. Stops drawing because of failing eyesight.

1952   *The Thurber Album, A New Collection of Pieces about
            People* is published by Simon & Schuster. *The Unicorn in
            the Garden* is filmed.

1953   *Thurber Country* is published by Simon & Schuster.
            Received honorary doctorate from Yale University and is
            awarded Sesquicentennial Medal by the Ohioana Library
            Association, Columbus.

1955   *Thurber's Dogs* is published by Simon & Schuster.

1956   *Further Fables for Our Time* is published by Simon &
            Schuster.

1957   *The Wonderful O* and *Alarms and Diversions* are pub-
            lished by Simon & Schuster and Harper & Brothers,
            respectively.

1958   Visits England. Becomes the first American since Mark
            Twain to be "called to the table" by the staff of *Punch*.

1959   *The Years with Ross* is published by Little, Brown and
            Company.

1960   Thurber joins the cast of "The Thurber Carnival" for 88
            performances.

1961   *Lanterns and Lances* is published by Harper & Brothers.
         Thurber sustains a blood clot 4 October and dies 4
         November. He is buried in Columbus, Ohio.

1962   *Credos and Curios* is published posthumously, by Harper
         & Row.

1980   *Selected Letters of James Thurber,* edited by Helen
         Thurber and Edward Weeks, is published by Atlantic,
         Little, Brown.

Conversations with James Thurber

Melancholy Doodler

Arthur Millier/1939

From *The Los Angeles Times Sunday Magazine*, July 2, 1939, pp. 6, 12, 17. Copyright © 1939, Los Angeles Times. Reprinted by permission.

As I shook hands with James Thurber I looked him straight in the eye and said that I understood he was quite, quite mad.

Well, maybe I didn't exactly say it out loud. Maybe what I really said was "Where and when were you born?" But so deft a psychologist as Thurber couldn't have missed the implication.

"Columbusohioeighteenninetyfour," he replied at more than Winchell speed. "That makes me forty-four. A terrible age. It scares me because there's only one way out—through the fifties. Heh heh. And I'm not mad."

He would pardon me, I said, but any consistent reader of the *New Yorker* knows quite well that James Thurber, America's ace creator of sophisticated screwy stories and equally screwy drawings, is mad.

Thurber's face lit up.

"Oh," he said, "so you know I also write?" There was genuine gratification in his voice.

I made a little mark in code on my cuff. It was point one in my projected analysis of Mr. Thurber's psyche. Translated, it meant: "Wife probably tells him he can't write."

"You are probably the only person in America who knows I write," he said bitterly. "They all say: 'Oh yes, Thurber?—the guy who makes those crazy drawings?' "

I was interviewing him on the sunny terrace overlooking the pool in Elliott Nugent's Bel-Air garden. Classmates at Ohio State University, Thurber was editor and Nugent associate editor of the college monthly, the *Sun Dial*, during the war. A confirmed telephone pad doodler, Thurber suddenly found himself without any staff artists. They were all in uniform. So he started printing his doodles in the *Sun Dial.*

But what was he doing in California?

3

"Elliott and I are writing a play together. For the New York stage. We hope Elliott can get away from Hollywood long enough to act in it next season."

I made another covert mark on the cuff. It translated: "Writing a play. Inferiority complex."

Behind double-lens glasses the tall, nervous Thurber was watching.

"I know what you're up to," he said, "you're psycho-analyzing me. Three of the country's foremost experts have offered to do it for nothing and I wouldn't waste their time. Why waste yours?

"Confidentially," he whispered, "it's not me that's mad. It's Harold Ross. Harold's mad. Wolcott Gibbs is mad. The whole New Yorker staff is mad—except me."

He leaned back luxuriantly in one of the Nugent terrace chairs and let the afternoon sunlight gild his wavy, graying hair and mustache.

Did I understand him to say that the entire New Yorker staff was mad from the managing editor down? I like to check startling statements, I explained.

"We always work that way on the New Yorker," he said. "Down. I was hired in 1929. Toward the end of the first week my secretary brought me the pay roll checks to sign.

" 'What's the idea,' I asked her. 'Why should I sign 'em?'
" 'Because you're the managing editor,' she said.

"That's the first I had heard of it," said Thurber. "But you get used to it. We counted up and found that the New Yorker has had 37 managing editors! Three of them are now office boys."

So he edited things, wrote stories—and doodled. One day he doodled a seal on a rock with Arctic explorers in the distance. His friend, E. B. White, picked the seal-doodle off the floor where Thurber had casually tossed it, inked it in and tried to peddle it to Ross as an illustration for the magazine. It came back with a sarcastic note appended and several marginal sketches by the art staff showing how a proper seal's whiskers should be drawn.

The sun was steadily dropping down the hill. Troops of brown, barefooted Nugent children appeared, stared, vanished. A handsome, tanned, smiling young man sauntered up. I could have sworn he was Robert Montgomery—but he called the equally young-looking Nugent "Pop." At any moment, now, I expected to see one of those melancholy menacing Thurber cave-woman in a short Greek shift come round a shrub with a stone club in her huge paw and threaten us. She would be Mrs. Thurber.

"White got sore," said Thurber, "and sent the seal back to Ross with an equally sarcastic note. It said: "This is how Thurber's seal's whiskers are drawn!" But Ross still had no use for it. I threw it away."

One day White took a thin manuscript to Harper and Sons with the electrifying title, "Is Sex Necessary?" Recognizing a vital question when they saw one, Harper's were all for publishing. But White made one condition. They must use the illustrations by one James Thurber.

"They looked at them," said Thurber, "then, making a great effort at politeness, they said: 'These are—er—the artist's rough ideas for the illustrations?' "

White assured Harper's that these were the finished jobs.

The book came out and the screwy drawings made a hit. "You see," said Thurber sadly, "that's the way life goes. I write stories with the utmost care, rewriting every one from three to 10 times. I have written so many of them for the *New Yorker* that six volumes of prose have already been published in book form to only one of drawings. Yet they say, 'Thurber? The bird who draws?' "

"I'm not an artist. I'm a painstaking writer who doodles for relaxation. But its those doodles they go for. Do you wonder I think it's a screwy world?"

He looked around furtively and, I thought, a bit scared.

"They've even labeled me a Dadaist and a surrealist. When the Museum of Modern Art put on its big exhibit of fantastic art they had a bunch of my drawings right on the tail end. Can I help it if I doodle?"

People talked so much about the drawings for *Is Sex Necessary?* that Harold Ross decided Thurber had been holding out on him. Why had he submitted no more drawings? "That one with the seal in it," he said. "I okayed that a year ago. Where is it?"

Thurber reminded him.

"Well, do it over again," said Ross. "We've got to have it."

Drawing things over is not Thurber's strong point, but he tried. He got the seal all right with the foolish expression and the whiskers. But when he got to the rock the darn thing began to look like a bed. "Why not?" he said. "If a rock prefers to be a bed, who am I to thwart it?"

When it was finished, the drawing showed a man and wife in bed. Behind them, on the headboard, was the seal. His caption had the weary husband burying his head for sleep and saying:

"Have it your way—you heard a seal bark."

That combination of goofy picture and caption started a wider fame for Thurber and suggested the title for his first book of drawings: *The Seal in the Bedroom.*

"Captions can make a drawing," said Thurber. "Some of my drawings lie around the office for years—waiting for an inspired line."

He writes most of his own, but E. B. White, whose mind runs in the same direction, thinks up some of them too. White's best-known caption—"I say it's spinach and the hell with it"—was inspired by another artist's *New Yorker* picture.

Mothers all over the country send drawings made by their bright young offspring to the magazine, pointing out that they are much better than Thurber's.

"And who knows," he says. "Maybe they are."

"Here's another funny thing. I almost never have a piece of writing turned down. They print them all—but who reads them? Whereas my drawings—the things people know me for—are often turned down. Terrific arguments go on between Ross and me before they get published."

The people in Thurber's drawings are a breed of his own discovery. Before he drew them nobody ever saw such creatures in real life. But now, once you see them, you recognize your own friends. Maybe—if you are very honest—yourself.

They are a bewildered looking lot. The women are more powerful than the men whom they perpetually push around. The women drive the cars, make the decisions, spout the culture. The men mostly just endure. Massive dogs sit on their haunches watching like poker-faced critics. The occasional child throws tantrums or poses unanswerable questions.

These people are intellectually a cut above the funny paper types. The man can wear dinner coats. The women would not be out of place on women's club rostrums, at symphony concerts, at literary teas. They are not the well-fed aristocrats of Peter Arno's cartoons, but the well-intentioned, upper half of the great middle class which in the cramped quarters of city apartments or the neat rows of suburbia, cherishes, rather pathetically, its pretensions to "the cultural things of life."

When Thurber begins a drawing of these curious yet strangely familiar people, he rarely knows what they will look like or do. He just lets his hand move with a pencil in it. His people simply happen, but they invariably have a family resemblance. They are done in thin, shaky lines without one touch of color. You can't imagine them without clothes. They never act. They only react.

Thurber's writing and drawing is a highly civilized variety of subtle criticism couched in nonsense terms. It fits somewhere between Aesop's fables and the nonsense poems and pictures of Edward Lear. It is brother to the work of his contemporaries, Ogden Nash, E. B. White and Ted Cook. It never aims to tell people what they should do. But it does make us look more closely at ourselves. It also makes us laugh.

He has characterized his kind of humorist thus: "They sit on the edge of the chair of literature. In the House of Life they have the feeling that they have never taken off their overcoats." As to what starts them going, he has written this: "The little wheels of their invention are set in motion by the damp hand of melancholy."

He was still sitting on the edge of the Nugent terrace chair—uneasily, I thought—and Nugent himself kept suggesting that I take a swim in his pool. Trying to get me away from Thurber, I suddenly realized. The handsome chap who looked the spittin' image of Robert Montgomery but called Nugent "Pop" kept going past with a fresh steak sandwich in one hand, a mug in the other. The sun was perilously low.

Just then a tall, pretty woman did come out from behind a shrub. She was Mrs. Thurber—Helen.

I made another code note on the cuff. It meant: "Helen—pretty but powerful."

"She edits all my stuff," Thurber said from his small mouth. "She used to write for the pulps. She really knows about writing."

All the analyst in me rose to a fine interrogation point. Hardly concealing my triumph, I jumped him with the question that would complete my great Thurber theory:

"She drives the car—and you can't drive!" I said—"Right?"

"Wrong," said Thurber. "I drive and she doesn't."

But there was a touch of melancholy in his voice as he said it. I believe he would rather have it the other way.

Then he uttered a terrible heresy. "Everybody thinks my characters are myself and my wife. They are not. I get my ideas from things people tell me or things I see others doing."

"Better have a swim," said Nugent for the sixth time. Perhaps Thurber was really getting dangerous and I didn't know it. But, no matter at what risk, newspapermen must get the news. "Tell me a few biographical facts," I said.

Mrs. Thurber came to his rescue. "I'm not his severest critic," she said. "His 8-year-old daughter is." One day she found three of his drawings of dogs.

"What are these?" asked little daughter.

"Dogs," said Thurber.

"Did you do them?"

"Yes," said their creator.

Daughter looked slowly, unenthusiastically, at each drawing.

"What for?" she said.

"Listen," said Thurber. "If you want my biography, look up the introduction E. B. White wrote for my book, *The Owl in the Attic*. It covers my known history very thoroughly down to the year 1931. If you want anything later than that, why not make it up yourself? It will save me the trouble." And he laughed the least melancholy laugh of the entire session as Nugent and the chap who looked like Robert Montgomery kindly but firmly dragged me toward the swimming pool.

I looked it up and it is a swell biography, as far as it goes. White explains that he first saw Thurber walking down the gangplank of a copra schooner in Raritonga, carrying a volume of Henry James and leading a honey bear on a small chain. And he went right on from there in a magnificent sweep of historical imagination.

I can't compete with that sort of brain. But just across the street I met a man from Manhattan who added a neat bit to the nebulous Thurber legend.

"They say in New York," he confided, "that when Thurber got really mad about something in the New Yorker office, instead of making a fuss or attacking somebody, he would step quietly to the distilled water dispenser, pick up the full five gallon bottle, carry it carefully to the center of the office, and let it fall smash on the floor.

"Then he would dust his long fingers together, place his hat squarely on the center of his long head, and go home."

That seems reasonable enough for a magazine plant where all the walls are on wheels and you have to hunt for your office in a fresh spot and shape every morning. (When I get back to the *Times* I'm going to look up our photo files. Maybe that really was Robert Montgomery!)

Thurber's Life and Hard Times

Robert van Gelder/1940

From *The New York Times Book Review,* May 12, 1940, p. 20.
Reprinted in van Gelder's *Writers and Writing* (New York: Charles
Scribner's Sons, 1946), pp. 52-55. Copyright © 1940 by The
New York Times Company. Reprinted by permission.

James Thurber said that when, in the mid-Nineteen Twenties, he
returned from France—where he had been working as a newspaper
reporter—he went round to Brandt and Brandt, the literary agency,
to ask whether the stuff he's been writing in his spare time had any
chance of publication.

"Some one there told me that I was most likely to sell to *The New
Yorker. The New Yorker* was about a year old but I'd never heard of
it. I went over to the magazine office with some thirty pieces. They
sent them all back. I wrote more and they sent those back. Then my
wife—my first wife—said that she thought I was spending too much
time on each piece; that I was worrying the life out of the ideas. I set
an alarm clock so that it would ring when I had worked on a piece for
forty-five minutes. I decided that was all the time I'd give myself on
each job.

"The first thing I wrote under that system not only sold—it caused
Ross (the editor) to send for me. I went to see him and in some way
or another Ross convinced himself that I was an old friend of Andy
White (E.B.W.). In fact, I'd met White only a few minutes before
meeting Ross.

"But because he liked my piece and because he thought I was a
friend of Andy's, Ross hired me. I started as managing editor, of
course—every one starts as managing editor on *The New Yorker.* I
didn't know that I was managing editor—I thought I was a writer. But
each week a girl would bring me slips of paper to sign and the third
week I asked her why I had to sign slips of paper. She explained that
these slips were the payroll and that signing them was part of my job.

"I went to Ross and told him that I didn't want to be managing
editor, that I wanted to write. He said, 'Nonsense!' He said that he

could get a thousand writers but good managing editors were hard to find. I could write if I wanted to but wouldn't be paid for it because my job was to be an editor and he wanted to discourage my writing. But I kept on turning out pieces and after quite a while Ross decided that since I was willing to write for nothing perhaps I was a writer after all."

He had been a member of *The New Yorker* staff for several years when one day E. B. White—they shared an office—picked up a drawing that Thurber had tossed toward the wastebasket and sent it in to *The New Yorker's* weekly art conference. The conferees thought this was whimsey and returned it. It was a picture of a seal—a penciled drawing on a piece of yellow copy paper.

White reinforced the lines with ink and again submitted the seal. Rejected a second time, the drawing was returned with an added sketch made by an artist at the conference and a note: "This is the way seal's whiskers look."

"Along about then Andy and myself wrote a book, *Is Sex Necessary?* And Andy insisted that my drawings be used as illustrations. Harper's weren't exactly fond of them, but when the book came out the drawings made a kind of hit. So the next time I met Ross he said: 'Say, why can't you give us some of your drawings?' "

Mr. Thurber hasn't stuck to his system of writing by the clock. When he goes to work on a piece he writes a first draft "just for size." "That draft isn't any good; it isn't supposed to be; the whole purpose is to sketch out proportions." He polishes this first draft, building up the material, perfecting the prose. The first page may be rewritten as many as fifteen times—not counting brief, warm starts. A passion for flawless typewriting causes him to recopy each page with a mistake on it, "and, of course, every time you copy a page you make changes."

Despite these labors, he enjoys the actual work of writing, he said.

"I rarely have a very clear idea of where I'm going when I start. Just people and a situation. Then I fool around—writing and rewriting until the stuff jells."

He is not doing any writing now. "I've had one bad eye for a long time and now I've a cataract on what was the good one. I can see that chair over there but I couldn't recognize any one in it." (The chair was about a yard away.)

He has learned that there are at least 300 varieties of cataract, named, like stars, for their discoverers. His, he said, is one of the simpler kinds, comparatively easy to be rid of, but two operations will be necessary. One this Spring and one in early Fall.

Tall and thin, with a pleasant voice, an exceptionally narrow mouth, a streak of white hair mounting from just above the ears. It is complimentary but true that neither in manner nor talk does he give indication of consciousness that he is a humorist with a reputation. No epigrams.

He commented that he is forty-five years old and that the forties are very hard going. He quoted John Jay Chapman, who said in his autobiography that he would have killed himself when in his forties except that he was sure he wasn't worth the powder and shot and the trouble of burial. Mr. Chapman reported that the fifties were better and Mr. Thurber hopes he was right.

"When you get to be forty-five the only thing you really want is another shot at the ten years since you were thirty-five, or better, at the fifteen years since you were thirty."

He was to fly to Bermuda the next morning, and some one who worked for the airplane company telephoned to make sure that Mr. Thurber knew what time the plane was to leave and where it was to leave from. Mr. Thurber returned to the interview not quite patient. "That's the third time they've called," he said. He feels that his reputation for being uncommonly vague and a little mad is not justified. His writing is based in truth distorted for emphasis and amusement—but truth. "It is reality twisted to the right into humor rather than to the left into tragedy."

The Male Animal, the play that he wrote with Elliot Nugent, "is fundamentally the story of the break-up of a marriage—but with a twist. If you told a friend that so-and-so and so-and-so had broken up, the friend would say, and mean it, 'That's too bad. I'm sorry.' But in the play we say, 'No, it isn't too bad. It is funny.' And we give it the twist that makes it funny.

"Some of the reviewers said that there were 'mad Thurber touches' in the play. You'd think if there were 'mad touches' I'd know about it. It all seems sane enough to me."

Mr. Thurber Observes a Serene Birthday

Harvey Breit/1949

From *The New York Times Magazine,* December 4, 1949, pp. 17, 78-79. Copyright © 1949 by The New York Times Company. Reprinted by permission.

James Thurber, whose compassionate satires and timely fables (both drawn and written) have made him America's most subtle and gifted humorist, will celebrate his fifty-fifth birthday on Thursday. He is completely philosophical about it.

Up in his room at a midtown Manhattan hotel, where he was breaking his trip from Hot Springs to his home in West Cornwall, Conn., Mr. Thurber, who gives the impression of being very gentle and very modest and highly impersonal and sensitized, revealed that he has not taken the years lightly. "Age," he said, "has been a terrific phobia with me. When I was 30, I felt that the next day I was going to be 40. When I was 40, I felt that the next day I was going to be 50. Now it is different. Now I think: I have five long years to 60."

Mr. Thurber got up from his chair, tall and thin, gaunt even, a figure disparate indeed from the race of short-statured, somewhat crushed-down, perplexed males he discovered and disclosed and made significant in his drawings. "When I was 34," Mr. Thurber continued, sitting down again, "I wrote a piece I called 'The Middle Years.' I had the fellow in it who was just my age—he was 34 too—practically a dodderer. Now I have got over my middle-age. I have gone past it into something better."

Certainly, as a writer, Mr. Thurber has never been better or more productive. In the past two years he has written more than forty pieces ("A hell of a lot more than I'd written in the five years before that") and is at work now on at least four projects; he likes to work on several things at a time, contrapuntally as it were.

This concentration which means riches for his readers is Mr. Thurber's way of compensating for the fact that he no longer draws. Mr. Thurber has not made a drawing in two years. "I have practically given up," he said.

13

Mr. Thurber took off his thick-lensed glasses and wiped his face with his handkerchief. "The doctors say I am stone-blind," he said. He has been undergoing a series of operations on his eyes—actually one protracted operation that was begun ten years ago. "All the apparatus by which a man sees, I don't have. Out of thirty thousand cases such as mine there are three that see. I'm one of the three.

"When I write now," he said with a startling and perfect kind of neutrality, "I am not handicapped by vision. I am undistracted by distraction—by the grass outside my window, or by flying birds.

"I used to be a writer who thought on the typewriter. My father had been with Underwood, and I knew how to typewrite by the time I was 6. Writers have wanted to run me out of town on a rail because I've said I like the physical business of writing on a typewriter. Now, I use a soft black pencil on yellow copy paper. I get about twenty words on a sheet. When I finish a short story it's about the size of a novel. I can't read those twenty words back. Fortunately, I have a good memory. (Given any two consecutive lines of *The Great Gatsby*, Mr. Thurber, who has read it only once, can, without any particular effort, tell you not only on what page the lines occur, but whether they appear on the top, bottom or middle of the page.) "Usually I get from 500 to 1,500 words in my mind before I start writing. Also I have shifted from being an eye-writer to being an ear-writer. Mrs. Thurber can read my unreadable hand, and reads what I've written back to me."

Mr. Thurber considered for a moment what he had said, and went on. "The greatest problem," he said, "is that I've had to give up reading. I have to be read to, and I fear I'll never get around to reading all the books I want to." Mr. Thurber says that being read to doesn't change the experience of reading. "Anything written well should read aloud," he said.

How much of a problem it was for Mr. Thurber to give up drawing it would be difficult to say; he talked about it absolutely naturally, without a tinge of martyrdom or pathos. "If all the lines of what I've drawn were straightened out, they would reach a mile and a half. I drew just for relaxation, in between writing."

The pacific and wonderful and wondrous hound who co-starred in Mr. Thurber's cartoons was a combination, he says of a prank, an accident and a real thing. "I had a friend who was on the telephone a great deal and while he talked he was always flipping the pages of his memo pad and writing things down. I started to fill up the pad with drawings so he'd have to work to get to a clean page. I began to draw a bloodhound, but he was too big for the page. He had the head and body of a bloodhound; I gave him the short legs of a basset. When I first used him in my drawings, it was as a device for balance: when I had a couch and two people on one side of a picture and a standing lamp on the other, I'd put the dog in the space under the lamp for balance.

"I've always loved that dog," said Mr. Thurber (echoing the sentiments of millions of Americans). "Although at first he was a device, I gradually worked him in as a sound creature in a crazy world. He didn't get himself into the spots that human beings get themselves into. Russell Maloney stated once that I believe animals are superior to human beings. I suspect he wanted to get me sore. If I have run down the human species, it was not altogether unintentional. They say that Man is born to the belief that he is superior to the lower animals, and that critical intelligence comes when he realizes that he is more similar than dissimilar.

"Extending this theory, it has occurred to me that Man's arrogance and aggression arises from a false feeling of transcendency, and that he will not get anywhere until he realizes, in all humility, that he is just another of God's creatures, less kindly than Dog, possessed of less dignity than Swan, and incapable of becoming as magnificent an angel as Black Panther.

"I have grown a little tired of the capitalization of Man, his easy assumption of a dignity more apparent than real, and his faith in a high destiny for which he is not fitted by his long and bloody history. The most frightening study of mankind is Man. I think he has failed to run the world, and that Woman must take over if the species is to survive."

Mr. Thurber was aware of having to explain a statement that seemed to contradict his drawings of the weaker vessel. "I think," he said, though with no suggestion of gallantry, "I've been misunderstood about women. The only catty letters I get are from men. They come from different men, but they all sound like the same man. Catty, and a little nasty—like clipping a drawing and writing on it 'Do you think this is funny?' The only anonymous letters I get are from

men. The only interesting letters I get are from women. The only
reason I draw women as savage is that they've failed to come up to
the level I think they can reach."

Mr. Thurber smoothed his hair, patted his face with his handkerchief, lit a cigarette, and said matter-of-factly: "I would like to see a
matriarchy. As a matter of fact, girls are bigger and stronger these
days, and most of them are wearing a size 10 shoe. Maybe nature is
working it out."

"The most alarming thing today," he said, apparently alarmed a
little that nature may not get a chance to work it out, "is that all the
kids are worried about the world situation. They didn't when I was
young. Then the greatest menace was Halley's comet. And my
Cousin Earl's motorcycle. They have things to worry about now."

Mr. Thurber thinks that the anxieties of today contribute to the
scarcity of humorists. "In the year 1930," he said, "Perelman published his first stories and Ogden Nash his first poems. All the rest of
the humorists got started in the Twenties. The depression had a much
more shattering effect on people than the first war. When a kid saw
his father come home in uniform, it seemed a natural thing. When a
kid heard his father say he was wiped out, and saw his mother burst
into tears, it was a shattering thing. There is a grim turn to the stories
today, even to humor. There were so many writers in the Twenties
without this sense of doom."

Even in the "lost generation" writers—Fitzgerald, Hemingway, Dos
Passos among them—Mr. Thurber thinks were without it. "The sense
of doom," he said, "that they had was more legendary than real.
They were the lost generation, but they were lost in Paris, and having
a pretty good time. All of them had a good twenty or thirty years to
look ahead to. There just wasn't the sense of another war to look
forward to then, as there is now."

Followers of Mr. Thurber's work see in his kindly and constant
hounds and his badgered human beings, his berserk situations and
his double-exposure wit, and number of talents and give to these any
number of names. But it is what one of Mr. Thurber's colleagues
termed his "grasp of confusion" that is the quintessence of Thurber.

When—in answer to an editorial ukase on the old Post, that the
staff write one-word, one-sentence, one-paragraph leads—Mr.

Thurber wrote: "Dead. That's what the man was the police found in an alley-way yesterday," his grasp of confusion ended the confusion.

The man who first inspired Mr. Thurber to write humor (and, as he says, "you probably haven't heard of him") is Robert O. Ryder, "the really great paragrapher of the *Ohio State Journal.*" He did a daily column for a quarter of a century and he would start it with a long paragraph and end it with a single line, Mr. Thurber's favorite being: "Women are either hearing burglars or smelling something burning." Mr. Thurber rates him among America's great humorists from Twain to E. B. White. Mr. Thurber, by the way, has never read *Tom Sawyer* or *Huckleberry Finn,* though he stated in a preface that he had even reread them. As he says, he wrote that in order to keep people from running him out of town.

Once Franklin D. Roosevelt delegated Mr. Thurber to serve the ends of confusion. It seems that during a lull in the Quebec Conference President Roosevelt, with his tongue in his cheek, told Mrs. Winston Churchill that Brussels sprouts was the great American vegetable, and that there were thirty-four interesting ways to cook Brussels sprouts. Mrs. Churchill was dubious, and the President decided on an elaborate joke. A few months before his death he told Mrs. Kermit Roosevelt he wanted to get out a privately printed pamphlet entitled "Thirty-four Ways to Cook Brussels Sprouts," and that he wanted Thurber to do the cover design (which he described in full detail: a long table holding a large glass bowl with Brussels sprouts that resembled the face of human beings, three separate lines of eager, smiling people, with forks in hands, converging on the table).

Mr. Thurber spent four afternoons trying to draw a Brussels sprout. The vegetable was out of season, so that he had none to feel; he couldn't visualize it; and the tear sheet he had of Brussels sprouts from a seed catalogue he couldn't see at all. A friend who was an artist and art teacher critically watched Mr. Thurber's efforts. "That is an electric light bulb," he would say, or "That is an apple," or "I don't know what that is."

Finally, the friend said, "think of a miniature squeezed baseball, seams and all." That did it. But here again Mr. Thurber demonstrated his "grasp of confusion": as the President had planned the cover, the design was a grim one; Mr. Thurber drew his dog in front of the table on his hind legs with one paw reaching for the bowl—which had the virtue of relieving a definitely macabre note. The pamphlet was privately printed for members of the Roosevelt and Churchill families. The artist never received a copy. But the joke was even funnier and more logical than the President could imagine: Vincent Sheean once mentioned Mr. Thurber's name to Winston Churchill, who, after groping a while, said, "Oh, yes, that insane and depraved artist."

One of Mr. Thurber's several going projects at this time is a parable of confusion. "It's a sort of fairy tale," he said, "that will run to about 12,000 words. It's called 'The Spoodle.' The story is placed in a country called Confusia. In it, everybody is suspected of the wrong thing. One person has seen the spoodle, another has heard it, and a third has even tasted it. The prosecutor is sure that the spoodle is un-Confusian and has to find it. If he can't find one, the prosecutor says, he will have to build one. It's a satire on the Un-American Committee's worst confusions. Enough hasn't been said, by the way, about the term un-American. Imagine saying un-Persian or un-Belgian."

One of Mr. Thurber's inoperative projects is a novel—something he is always beginning and which is always turning into a short story. "I once wanted to write a novel about Bernadette," he said, "until that book came along. I have a theory about Bernadette and her vision. There are certain kinds of spots-before-the-eyes that take definite shapes. They are scientifically called phosphenes. I have a bright blue shape these days—though it used to be brighter. It's always there, but you have to look for it." (Mr. Thurber looked for it and apparently located it.) "At one time my phosphenes used to take the definite shape of the face of Herbert Hoover. Of course, it wouldn't make history."

Columbus Still Home to Thurber; It's Locale of Latest Book

Bob Kanode/1950

From *Columbus* (Ohio) *Dispatch,* June 15, 1950, p. 4-A. Reprinted with permission of *The Columbus Dispatch.*

Although he has been in New York for more than 23 years, Columbus is still home to Jim Thurber, former *Dispatch* reporter, now famous as an author and magazine writer.

And the old home town will be the locale of the latest Thurber volume, scheduled for publication by Simon & Schuster in the fall of 1951. It will be entitled *Thurber Country.*

Jim, who was at the Deshler-Wallick Hotel Wednesday with his wife, Helen, still has about five chapters of the book to finish. Some have already been published in *The New Yorker.*

"You know, mother has about 5,000 relatives in and around Columbus and I've been tracing the family history back before the Civil War," Jim explained Wednesday.

The book will deal extensively with the Broad and High scene and many of the friends and associates of Thurber's university days at OSU such as Prof. Joseph Taylor. It will be illustrated with old family pictures, he declared.

Jim recently worked on some chapters of the book while in Bermuda and he also is working on an adult fairy tale to be entitled "The 13 Clocks."

Although he has not produced any of the famous Thurber pen drawings for the past three years, the former reporter is looking forward to taking up drawing again as soon as two mechanical devices now being perfected are made available to him.

One is an especially lighted drawing board being made by the General Electric Co. that carries its illumination from beneath the board.

The other is a mechanical pencil made of aluminum and manufactured in Czechoslovakia that produces a brilliantly lighted line that glows like neon tubing.

Both of these, Jim hopes, will eliminate the handicap of impaired eyesight, although Jim Thurber never for one moment let the eye difficulty slow him down.

Jim's amazing memory for dates and things serves him in good stead. He recalls that he left Columbus and the *Dispatch* in 1922, went to New York, got a job on the *New York Post*. He joined the *New Yorker* staff in 1927. Whether or not it was his arrival on the *Post* he laughingly recalls, but anyway, it wasn't long before the price of the paper was cut from 5 to 3 cents.

Jim tired of newspaper work later and went to France for a time. Paris was an old love with him because he had been a clerk in the American embassy there before coming back to the U.S. after World War I and joining the *Dispatch* staff.

Later he began writing articles for the *New Yorker* and his droll humor struck the national fancy. One of his most famous pieces was entitled "The Night the Bed Fell."

Jim Thurber and the writer were reporters together covering City Council meeting at the old City Hall in E. State St. on the site of the Ohio Theater on Jan. 13, 1921, when the building burned to the ground.

The newspapermen were intent on the Council meeting, called to discuss the ever turbulent "gas rate question." They were unaware the ancient pile was a seething mass of flames until firemen burst into the room yelling, "Get the hell out, don't you darn fools know the building is on fire."

Ever alert, Thurber grabbed a roll of blue prints of some alley paving project and carried it with him as he fled to the street. The next morning there appeared in the *Dispatch* a graphic story about the "valuable papers" saved from the roaring flames by the heroic reporter.

Jim keeps in close touch with his mother, Mrs. Charles Thurber, still amazingly alert and active although she is now near the 85 mark. His brothers Bob and Bill are also here in Columbus and all reside at the Southern Hotel.

Jim came back to Ohio this time to receive the honorary degree of Doctor of Letters at Kenyon College—his first degree. Although active at Ohio State University and prominent in campus activities there he did not graduate—the lure of Paris and the embassy job were greater.

But, Jim did write several plays for Scarlet Mask, the campus theatrical society. He and Elliott Nugent became famous for their playwright work.

Now, after a lapse of 10 years he and Nugent are again working together on a production. In all, he has written 16 books, has nearly finished the 17th and two more three-quarters and half done respectively.

Besides *Thurber Country* and *The 13 Clocks* he is writing *Thurber People* and "The Spoodle," the latter being 10,000 words satire on congressional investigations and red probes.

A prophet without honor in his own country to some degree, Thurber regards the rumors that he has been discussed, then turned down, for honorary degrees at Ohio State University as somewhat amusing.

The unfailing sense of Thurber humor has carried the former reporter through many a situation that would make another man despondent—many illnesses, the loss of an eye through an unfortunate "William Tell" episode with another brother when he was a youngster, failing sight in the other eye, the death of his father and other situations.

Jim could see humor where others saw nothing but dignity or at least conditions that required one to be serious. In the days before Columbus got its river front city hall, part of the city offices were quartered temporarily for several years on the second floor of the Public Library at Grant Ave. and State St.

As in all libraries, silence was the golden rule and two situations intrigued Thurber. One was the fact that Bert Killam, then secretary of the Civil Service Commission, played in a band and parked his tuba in his office.

The other was that Leroy Rose, an assistant city clerk for years, longed for the brassy clamor of an ancient fire gong that operated in the old State St. city hall.

Finally the time came—when Killam's office was vacant. Jim sneaked in, extracted the huge tuba from its case, blew several resounding blasts on it, slapped the horn back in its case and fled.

Shocked lady librarians flew up the marble stairs to remonstrate with uncouth city officials who sought to turn their sedate atmosphere into an African tribal dance.

Naturally, no one knew anything about the blasts and officials were as mystified as were the ladies.

Thurber did this more than once until finally someone detected the cause of the reverberating toots and made Killam keep his tuba away from the Thurber reach.

If Leroy Rose wanted fire alarms clanging in his ear Thurber could see no reason why he shouldn't have them—library or no library—he wrote long and burning articles about the situation, suggested Indian tom-toms, Turkish cymbals, rattle bones and other media for satisfying the Rose yearning—all to no avail.

Of course, from time to time, Thurber would lay hands on old tire tools, brass cuspidors and other hardware to give out his own version of the fire alarm effect. The reaction from the library was the same, only more vigorous—they threatened to give Thurber the library version of the "bum's rush."

The Thurber legend would require volumes to tell and the author's 84-year-old mother is as sharp-witted as her son.

Jack Hutton, *Dispatch* photographer, was taking pictures of the family in their suite at the Southern. Sitting on a bed, the elder Mrs. Thurber turned to her daughter-in-law, Helen, and remarked:

"It's good of them to be taking such pains to have nice pictures. The papers always like to have them on hand in case somebody dies!"

"What an idea," laughed Helen. She is a Nebraska girl who went to New England when she was one and thus has lived most of her time in the east.

Aside from his wife and mother, Jim has two brothers, Bob and Bill who also live at the Southern. Jim's dad, Charles L. Thurber, for many years secretary to Mayor James A. Thomas, died on Easter Sunday of 1939.

In connection with his work on "Thurber People," Jim is especially anxious to learn little stories and anecdotes about his old friend of OSU, Prof. Joseph R. Taylor. They can be sent to his mother, Mrs. Mary Agnes Thurber at the Southern. She will forward them to her son.

Jim has a daughter, now 18, who is interested in the stage and it will probably be no surprise to have an announcement come from New York that Jim himself has taken to treading the boards in an original comedy drama of life like that of his comic characters in his famous drawings.

Thurber: Man or Golux?

Lewis Gannett/1950

From *Harper's Bazaar*, November, 1950, pp. 130, 190. Copyright
© 1950. The Hearst Corporation. Courtesy of Harper's Bazaar.

If you read James Thurber's new fairy tale, which will be out this
month, you may understand what I mean by saying that he is a
Golux. The Golux in *The Thirteen Clocks* says, "Half the places I
have been to never were. I make things up. Half the things I say are
there cannot be found."

If I said that Thurber was also the prince in his fairy story—"A
thing of shreds and patches, a ragged minstrel singing for pennies
and the love of singing"—you might fairly reply, as the Duke did
when Hark talked of the clockwork in a maiden's heart that strikes
the hours of youth and love, "Chocolate chatter!" Maybe it is chocolate chatter, but it's Thurber. Thurber is a thoroughly unreliable and
quite nonsensical character, who delights almost equally in violating
rules and remembering birthdays. He hates mankind and likes almost
everybody he ever met, except when he is engaged in cursing his
dearest friends. He wrote *The Thirteen Clocks* in Bermuda, where he
had gone to write another book. He is usually writing some other
book from the one he thinks he is writing, and sometimes several
others.

He is blind and not at all resigned to being blind. The occasions
when he hates his best friends are usually occasions when a friend
has tried to help him find his way about an unfamiliar room or has
tiptoed around the subject of blindness. His blindness, Thurber often
says, is the most important thing in his life and naturally he likes to
talk about it. At other times he will exclaim with equal vehemence
that his blindness has nothing whatever to do with his character, his
writing or his drawing; and anyway, he isn't totally blind. He has one-
ninth vision in one eye, especially just after sundown.

It began when Thurber was six. His brother shot him in the eye
with an arrow. Thurber was impatient even at six. It had been

planned that his brother was to shoot him in the back to see if it hurt, but Jamie was as always impatient, and just as his brother drew the bow, Jamie looked around to see what was happening. If the wounded eye had been removed at once, Thurber says—and he considers himself, and he probably is, an authority on opthalmology—the other eye might have been saved. Instead, it too became infected, and has defied medical authorities ever since. When Thurber was in his forties, the authorities thought they might improve it by operation. They operated five times and it didn't improve, and then they said Thurber would lose all vision.

Characteristically, he and his eye refused to obey the authorities. He even thinks the eye may be improving, which would be medically impossible apart from the fact that Thurber is Thurber. At any rate, after three years in which Thurber didn't draw a single dog, even on a blackboard—which in the days of sinking vision had been his substitute for drawing paper—he has begun to draw again. Tom Torre Bevins, production manager for Thurber's publishers, meditated on the blackboard story and one day brought Thurber samples of various types of black paper, and luminous white crayons. With these, further aided by a sort of eyeshade long-range microscope called a "Zeiss Loop," Thurber, just after sunset on clear days, is drawing again.

He says he doesn't care whether he draws or not and insists that his blindness has made no difference in his memory or his writing. His psychology professor discovered when Thurber was in college (Ohio State) that he had a phenomenal memory, and Thurber doesn't think that it is any better today than it was then. He can and gladly will quote, if encouraged, whole paragraphs of Henry James's most complicated sentences, and one of his favorite sports is remembering his friends'—and enemies'—birthdays and ages. Some of them say that he has been known to err, but he doesn't remember that.

He resents his blindness for a variety of reasons, but he is most eloquent about it when explaining that blindness makes sin extraordinarily difficult. (The Golux, you will read, had hopes of being evil until he came upon a firefly burning in a spider's web. Maybe Thurber did too.) Thurber thoroughly enjoys all of his amazingly versatile resentments and particularly resents the fact that he enjoys them so much. He would like to hate the world far more than he quite can.

Whether or not Thurber's infected eye had anything to do with the unique perspective on seals, dogs and human beings exhibited both in his drawings and in his prose—and Thurber will, at least on occasion, hotly deny that it had—there is no doubt that his perspective has always been unique and grows uniquer. (The grammarians may tell you that there is no such grade as "uniquer," but then, no grammarian was ever a Golux.) It is quite possible that, sitting alone in the dark, gazing at the spots before his eye, he sees things that two-eyed people do not see, and certainly the darkness has sharpened his senses of both hearing and touch. Even Thurber will admit that.

He defines people in terms of voice, sometimes with clairvoyance. He has been known to predict a marital breakup before the spouses themselves suspected it and to declare that he had discerned it by tones of voice. His fingers are always at work, feeling; they are never still. And no writer of our day is more sensitive to the rhythms and cadences of words. He doesn't see what he writes; he hears it. He writes, as a rule, longhand—fifteen or twenty words sprawling across and sometimes overlapping on big sheets of yellow paper, and then he has it read back to him, sometimes as many as twenty times, amending and rephrasing as he listens. Much of *The Thirteen Clocks* is considerably more precise poetry than most modern poets write.

In the old days, Thurber says, he was "typewriter-bound." He could not write unless he could see what he was writing. Now he listens before he writes and listens again after he writes, and he writes better and better with every book. *The Thirteen Clocks* is the best thing he has *ever* done. There was a time when critics thought of Thurber as merely another *New Yorker* humorist. Gradually it has been dawning on them that he is about the most exquisitely frustrated creative artist with words in our day, writing in a form that is ever-changing and all his own.

The Golux was "something very much like nothing anyone had seen before"; and he "made things up." Thurber made the Golux, and the Golux is Thurber.

Breakfast with Thurber

Joseph Deitch/1951

From *The Christian Science Monitor,* August 9, 1951, p. 11.
Reprinted by permission from *The Christian Science Monitor.* ©
1951 by The Christian Science Publishing Society. All rights
reserved.

It is easy to picture James Thurber as a character in his own book—in
The Thirteen Clocks, for instance, his latest fairy tale. At breakfast at
the Algonquin here the other morning he was found to be a very tall,
flatly structured man—reedy, with a look of the Eiffel Tower on a hazy
day about him. He looms, rather than stands, in front of you, and he
is apt to sway in the wind.

His immediate impact on one is not hilarious, although he says it
isn't true that humorists are sad at heart. Mr. Thurber takes his humor
seriously. As a writer he is a perfectionist. He feels that the longer you
work on your stuff, even after it is presumably finished, the better it
becomes. Consequently he hates to turn in a manuscript. He would
like to putter with it indefinitely—cutting, adding, polishing, or just
brooding constructively over it.

He rewrote *The Thirteen Clocks* 22 times. It had to be taken from
him almost by force—it got to the point, he says, where he was
merely "having fun tinkering with clocks and running up and down
secret stairs."

Thurber is a gentle, soft-chuckling sort of fellow who, at most,
looks every second or third inch a humorist. He is heavily spectacled,
half white-haired and strangely, inevitably, youthful, with a wispy
mustache. His leisurely manner does not betray the depth and wis-
dom one senses in the man. All in all, he is probably what an urban
fairy-tale and fable writer ought to look like in the middle of the
twentieth century.

It is safe to say, however, that a scholarly child might take him for a
compiler of literary sub-treasuries, or dean of a small liberal arts college, or possibly as someone distinguished in the professions requir-
ing a pith helmet—as a lean and silent jungle explorer, perhaps,

or an Egyptologist. Average children, the kind who want to be jet pilots or television script writers, will be reminded of somebody pleasant in Grimms', Andersen's and certainly Thurber's fairy tales, and let it go at that.

There was a temptation to ask Mr. Thurber if his middle name is Stringfellow. It could be, but you aren't surprised to learn it's Grover, and that he was born near Cleveland.

The Algonquin's waiters, cool, precise men, who may well be contributors to the *Yale Review*, seemed to know Mr. Thurber for what he really is—the author of some of the best light prose in our literature, a former newspaperman, a friend. And they served him lovingly. He was, in fact, the monarch returned to the realm that morning.

He and Mrs. Thurber get down to New York from Connecticut about once a month. He reported that one of his acquaintances in town has been trying to read deep, or double, meaning into his fairy tales, or at least into *The Thirteen Clocks,* something that saddens him. He wrote the latter in Bermuda simply "as an example of escapism," and because he feels that "modern man ought to wander down the byways of fantasy once in a while."

He may also, of course, have been enchanted by three elves on the island, named Sara Linda, Ronnie and Janey Williams. (Sara Linda, aged four, "insisted on oleanders in the Princess's hair; instead of freesias, and there were several grueling conferences about this from which I barely emerged the winner.") Besides, most writers want to do a fairy tale sometime.

"People today seem to want to escape into, or hide in, television," it occurred to Mr. Thurber as he buttered his toast. "Television is going to cut into reading, which can be an intelligent form of escape."

Did he have a special audience in mind for his story?

"All children over ten will like it," he guessed, although Simon & Schuster, its publisher, rather neutrally call it a fairy tale, parable or poem for children and adults.

Told that his more established writing is beginning to be read in some eighth-grade English classes as an example of the "humorous essay," Mr. Thurber beamed, then frowned.

"As an example of the essay?" he wondered. "It's more, I suppose, what the *New Yorker* calls the casual. A casual is anything that's not strictly fact and under five thousand words. Anything that's—well, casual," he added, and a momentary pause may have been used to consider the possibility of such textbook questions on his work as: "Do you think Thurber would be fun to know? Explain."

"By the way," he recalled, brightly, "when I was a reporter for the *Columbus Dispatch,* in Ohio, I was also the city's correspondent for the *Christian Science Monitor.* I enjoyed the job, including the checks from Boston made out to Jane Thurber."

Mr. Thurber remembers his newspaper experience with high affection. He is devoted to the papers he worked for as a young man, and when he goes home he usually drops in on them to see old friends. He likes reading thoughtful articles about himself, and has found that small-town reviews of his books are often more interesting than the major ones. His mother—"one of the most magnificent persons I have ever known"—and two brothers still live in Columbus.

With the recent publication in the *New Yorker* of the first parts of "The Thurber Album," his work may be said to have entered its nostalgic, or reminiscent period. He is here writing of people and situations in his family history, as he remembers them and as revealed by research. It should not be likened to "Fables for Our Time," which are largely ficitious accounts of odd predicaments his family got into when he was a boy, such as the day the dam broke and the night the bed fell on his father.

"The new articles are based on fact—they're true," Mr. Thurber explained. "I find myself rewriting them every two weeks or so, because I keep finding out things about those times."

Mr. Thurber had a those-were-the-days look in his eye.

"Those were indeed the days," he mused, adding that "all the graceful things I remember are gone, like presenting your calling card to the maid. Most people long for these things, deep down.

"Why are historical novels so popular today, and notice, too, the revival of Henry James. There's a book in every family," he went on, "in every person, in mothers, fathers, children, the front yard, the dog, the porch—"

Amid the bright hotel chatter and the traffic outside, you suddenly understood a lot about James Thurber and the spirit of his album.

Talk with James Thurber
Harvey Breit/1952

From *The New York Times Book Review*, June 29, 1952, p. 19.
Reprinted in Breit's *The Writer Observed* (Cleveland and New
York: The World Publishing Co., 1956, p. 256). Copyright ©
1952 by The New York Times Company. Reprinted by permission.

This column, in order that it get written, requires (in the language of
the fourth state) a news peg. Once a week, presumably, an author is
in the news: he has written a book, or he has come back from a long
journey, or he has a novel opinion about civil liberties or a civil opinion about novels. For this column's safety-deposit holdings, though,
no new peg is required to have a talk, even a formal talk, with James
Grover Thurber. As luck would have it, though, there turned out to
be three news pegs to justify (where no justification was required) a
talk with Jim Thurber. Mr. Thurber has a new book out, *The Thurber
Album* (it has made the best-seller chart); Mr. Thurber, together with
collaborator Elliot Nugent, has *The Male Animal* once again tickling
the collective ribs of the playgoing mobs; and Mr. Thurber has
returned to America after 100 days of absence.

On the 101st day, that is on the first day back, Mr. and Mrs. Thurber had lunch at their usual midtown hotel. One by one the men who
help make the *New Yorker* a brilliant magazine came by and greeted
Mr. Thurber, remarked on his stay, congratulated him on his play and
on his book. Then the various maîtres came over and welcomed him.
Finally the waiters who weren't waiting on his table came over and
saluted him. It was a tribute that Mr. Thurber took head bowed, as it
were, and muttering with pleasure and embarrassment into the table.
The 57-year-old Mr. Thurber, as a matter of fact, looks well—though
he has lost some weight which he can ill afford to lose. His face was
healthy burned and he looked rested. "I ought to look rested," Mr.
Thurber said, "I didn't do a damn thing."

Being an old hand at reporting Mr. Thurber decided to help along.
"About the book," he began, "you can say it's about Taft county but

it's by an Eisenhower man." Mr. Thurber, thinking on politics and the state of the Union, took a jump or two. "If we don't stop suspecting all writers," he said, "it will be a severe blow to our culture. I think all writers, even the innocent ones, are scared. There's guilt by association, guilt by excoriation, there's guilt by everything the politicians invent. And it's rather foolish to hold the respect we do for ex-Communists, that is, people who once tried to overthrow the Government. Pretty soon some new Budenz will drop out of The Party deliberately, and we will go ahead and make him a hero."

Just about that time Elliot Nugent visited briefly, and when he left, Mr. Thurber picked up the thread of the discussion. "People ask why there isn't a comedy like *The Male Animal* any more—something that's free and exuberant. It isn't possible to write a comedy like that any more because we're living in the most frightened country in the world. How confusing my dossier must be. I wouldn't join a Communist organization, obviously. But I won't be scared off those organizations I did sign up for. They say now—it's gotten so abject—don't join anything. Don't even join a garden club."

None of it was funny. Mr. Thurber wasn't feeling funny. Still, Mr. Thurber ought to talk about humor, oughtn't he? "Humor isn't considered one of the major arts," Mr. Thurber said after the briefest pause. "The best essay on humor I know was written by Andy White in 'A Subtreasury of American Humor.' I guess books of humor don't last because, like the passions, humor is a changing thing. It is likely to date because it deals in the modern idiom. I wonder about *Babbitt*, whether the humor in that wouldn't date? According to Mencken," Mr. Thurber said, "There are only two American novels, *Babbitt* and *Huck Finn*. The best estimate of my work was done by T. S. Eliot."

Mr. Thurber shook his head affirmatively. "Most humorous books date and the serious books don't," he said. "When you see *As You Like It* you know it was written over 250 years ago." What about a book like *Tristram Shandy*? "I haven't tried those old books. I can't get through *Pickwick Papers*. And don't forget, there's a cult around the old work which makes it difficult to know when it's funny and when it's supposed to be funny. I can't remember any humor in old Scott Fitzgerald. Humor would have saved him. It seems to me the great novelists have humor in them, even if it isn't predominant. The Russians had it; Gogol had it, and Dostoevsky. It seems to me

Fitzgerald strangled humor because he was caught in the romantic tradition. Well, there isn't a trace of humor in communism, is there? I think any political system that vehemently attacks humor reveals a great weakness. It is one of the dangers universally. One of the great things we have here is humor—even in war. We ought not to lose that."

May Take 1000 Years—
Says Superwomen Will Force Peace
The Associated Press/1953

From *The Columbus Dispatch,* Sunday, August 23, 1953, p. 7.
Reprinted with permission of The Associated Press

EDGARTOWN, MASS., AUG. 22—(AP)—Humorist James Thurber, who says he isn't kidding, thinks a race of superwomen eventually will achieve world peace by forcing men to cease their warring. But this, unfortunately, may take 1000 years.

"I consider the American women the greatest potential power in the world and altogether too complacent and lazy to do anything about it," the 58-year-old cartoonist, writer-playwright told me. In the next breath, he'll tell you he loves women.

"People have the impression I dislike women," he said. "That is entirely wrong. I always praise women highly. We get along fine.

"All my life I have been surrounded by females. I have a female wife, a female 21-year-old daughter who was married last February, a female cook, and a female dog. I have always owned female dogs. I was brought into the world by a female doctor.

"When I had a nervous breakdown I consulted a woman psychiatrist. I have written Prefaces to four books by women. A man who hated women surely would not go to that trouble."

Thurber, on vacation there, talked of this race of superwomen this way:

"Nature, as you know is making women larger all the time. Their feet are bigger, they are taller and broader every generation. After another 1000 years of this evolution, during which man will lag far behind, women will be able to establish what man has failed to do in all the years of the 2800 Years War—a lasting peace."

About that 2800 Years War; What do you mean by that?

"People," Thurber says, "make the mistake of thinking there have been separate wars. Actually the world has been at war for at least 2800 years. The first Punic War, the 30 Years War, the 100 Years

33

War, the War of 1812, the Boer War, World Wars I and II and all the rest are only skirmishes of the 2800 Years War. That's the name I've given it.

"Wars will never stop until the creative sex, which instinctively hates war, takes charge. Some guy, a scientist, said in a book called *Social Life of Animals,* that man is the only species from the slug and the potato bug to the elephant, that seeks to destroy its own kind. That is the driving impulse of the mob.

"Since women haven't the ambition to become mentally and morally strong enough to straighten out the world, they will have to become physically strong enough to do it. That will take another 1000 years.

"Wouldn't I just love to be alive to see it! What a sight it will be when any woman can belt her husband clear across the room and tell him the place for the little man is in the kitchen and he'd better stay there if he knows what's good for him.

"Why, men won't be allowed to carry guns or sharp-edged weapons—or even matches to make sure they won't be able to hurt each other."

What a day, gals!

Thurber Has His Own Brand of Humor

John Ferris/1953

From *The Columbus Citizen*, November 8, 1953.

NEW YORK, NOV. 7—In the critical days following an operation, James Thurber observed quietly, a woman worries about her hair. A man, in the post-operative stage, doesn't think about his barber, but a woman thinks about her hairdresser.

"A man," said Mr. Thurber, "is indifferent or he doesn't remember. A woman never forgets. A woman goes into a restaurant, and she is thinking that all the other women are saying, 'Look at her. She hasn't had her hair done in 23 days.' Or it may be 15 days or 34 days. A woman always knows to the day, and she assumes other women do, too."

Mr. Thurber settled himself in a wing chair, lighted a cigarette and ran his long, thin fingers resolutely through his long, thick hair. He was explaining the absence from their Algonquin Hotel suite of his wife, Helen, who, having undergone an operation for a detached retina on Aug. 20, had withstood with admirable fortitude the temptation to go at once to her hairdresser.

"This was the 48th day and she went," he said.

"If a bomb ever hits New York," he said, "the men will be beating it out of town, and the women will be running around to see if their hairdresser's shop was hit."

There was neither derision nor scorn in his voice. He was stating a fact, a Thurber fact, garnished delicately with the Thurber humor which his friend, the late Stephen Vincent Benét, himself a distinguished poet, once defined as a definite and conscious distortion of reality.

Now Mr. Thurber, grateful that his wife was rapidly recovering from her operation, was marking time to the publication of his 20th book, *Thurber Country*, and working on another, "The Sleeping Man," which is due in the spring.

Thurber Country is a collection of pieces, dating from 1949, from

35

the *New Yorker, Holiday, Cosmopolitan* and the *Bermudian,* a
monthly edited by a friend. The title had been intended for another
book published five years ago. It had been picked from a list of 50
suggested titles, but at the last minute there was a switch to "The Best
in Me."

"The Sleeping Man," a satire on the anxieties of the American
male, is a long narrative begun this past spring in Williamsburg, Va.,
where the Thurbers spent six weeks before going to Martha's Vineyard. Tourists swarmed through Williamsburg when the Thurbers
were there. But Mr. Thurber found the mood of the old capital,
restored by Rockefeller millions, peaceful and reassuring.

It was comforting to think of placid Colonial Williamsburg and its
gracious living, and it was impossible not to contrast it with the appre-
hensive reality of 1953.

So the narrative began, taking the form of a dream, and, although
Mr. Thurber has never read Kafka's *The Castle* or *The Trial*, he has a
fair notion of the later novel and expects the inevitable comparisons.
(He has had parts of Joyce's *Finnegans Wake* read to him by a secretary who was baffled but unbroken by the twilight language.)

"I always work better out of town," Mr. Thurber said, "I started
The 13 Clocks in Bermuda, and *The White Deer* in Hot Springs. I
don't find it easy to work in New York. I used to do my work here by
going over to the *New Yorker* office late at night and just working. I
don't work by the clock. I have no rules, I don't set myself so much
work to do and do it."

Life magazine once sent a photographer to make some pictures of
Mr. Thurber. The photographer brought along a large dial with a
clock device and explained to Mr. Thurber that he wished to time his
drawing a picture. Mr. Thurber says:

"I sat down and he fixed the clock. I drew a man, a woman, a
table, lamp and a dog and looked up. I'd done the picture in 72
seconds. The photographer quickly put the thing away. 'Guess we
can't use this,' he said."

Mr. Thurber's beginnings as a comic artist on the *New Yorker* were
as difficult as his start as a writer. Only E. B. White really was enthu-
siastic about his drawings because Thurber had illustrated *Is Sex
Necessary?* which they had written together.

Eventually, Editor Harold Ross saw the drawings through White's eyes and they were an instantaneous hit. Mr. Thurber has worked on a play about Ross and the *New Yorker* since 1947 and may still finish it. He puts it this way:

"Ross is dead. This would be a tribute to him."

The blindness which has been with him since 1940 has not impaired his production. On the contrary, he has worked harder. Lately he has virtually abandoned the drawing which gave him rank as a comic artist, though he thinks of resuming it, possibly when he and Mrs. Thurber go to their country home at West Cornwall, Conn.

"Actually, I can't see a 72-point (one inch) headline," he said. "And when I write, I write 20 words to the page. One of my short story manuscripts looks like a novel."

He became blind in one eye at the age of 6 when his brother shot him with a toy arrow. The vision of the other eye was affected, and in 1940 he underwent a series of operations. This put an end to his work at the typewriter, and he had to learn to dictate.

"I was a visual writer, but I never learned the touch system. I liked the shape of words and phrases, and I liked clean copy. I never turned in a page with a single mistake on it. I always copied it over. Naturally, when you copy you make changes and you improve your copy.

"Scott Fitzgerald once said to Thomas Wolfe, 'I'm a taker out and you're a putter in. That's our difference.' Of course, you can see it when you compare *The Great Gatsby* hard, polished, economical, with the great softness, the turgidity of Wolfe. Well, I'm a taker out myself."

It took two years for him to dictate easily. Now he generally composes about 1500 words in his head before he dictates. He is not distracted by things which distract writers who see. He doesn't stare out of the window or at the bowl of fruit or the water pitcher.

He thinks out stories, dictates to a secretary, and she reads the work back. He corrects there. He still writes descriptive parts of times, but he likes to dictate dialogue.

He has a prodigious memory for dates. He doesn't flaunt his power, observing modestly that a man remembers or he doesn't.

Listening to him, you become aware that he inserts dates in his stories with no effort: He sailed for Europe in 1925 on such-and-such a date. Got his job on the Paris edition of the *Chicago Tribune* on this

date, his *New Yorker* job on another. He remembers birthdays, odd
telephone numbers, etc.

Other students at Ohio State University marveled at the Thurber
memory. When a professor of psychology recited 500 words and
asked his class to repeat them, Mr. Thurber frequently hit 80 per cent
of the words while the rest of his class did no better than 17 per cent.

He remembers the birthdays of at least 300 friends, the birthday of
a girl he was in love with in the third grade (Oct. 9, 1894) and his old
Columbus telephone number (2166).

But in writing the pieces that make up *The Thurber Album* he
wrote over 500 letters over a four-year period and had researchers
dig out and confirm his own dates and remembrances of things past.

He is concerned with the dearth of young humorists, recalling that
in the 1920s "humorists were a dime a dozen," and he named a few:
S. J. Perelman, Corey Ford, Frank Sullivan, Ogden Nash, Spud
Johnson, Arthur Kober, Dorothy Parker, Sally Benson, E. B. White.

"No one has come along to take their place. The depression did
something to us. The kids became serious after 1930. The colleges
don't turn out men who write humor. All the ones I named have
been working for years."

He talks of his blindness with serene dispassion and of his drawings
with disarming casualness. He marvels at the advance in medicine,
pointing out that on two occasions the so-called wonder drugs saved
his life. And he is deeply touched by the sympathy and advice—most
of the advice is valueless—of people the world over.

"I'll tell you something that is hard to believe when we think of all
the cruelty and selfishness in the world. Ten men in the United States
and one in England, strangers to me, have offered me an eye in the
belief they could help me. But an eye cannot be transferred."

People have written him to watch Mexican jumping beans to improve his vision, to have his spine rubbed, to use lemon juice, to use
a hot flatiron against the side of his face. He is appreciative because
he knows the suggestions are made in good faith. "Laymen are more
ignorant of the eye than any other part of the body. The eye is an
unbelievably delicate instrument. Yet it is also strong. You read in bad
light and tire your eye muscles. You rest and the eye is as good as
new."

"There's one thing I'd like to tell you to write," he said. "One of the worst things that can happen to a child, an accident affecting its eyes, can and does happen because parents are careless. A woman hands a cat to a child to keep the child occupied while the mother works. When a child plays with a cat it should always be given some bright object, a spoon or a small pan—anything bright—to hold between itself and the cat. Cats strike out at anything that gleams. Children's eyes pick up light and the cat is likely to strike swiftly and may injure the child's eyes."

Mr. Thurber loves dogs, but he knows that dogs can be dangerous around small children, too. A jealous dog can be terrible, he says. He has a few rules of his own which he passes along to friends:

"If there is an old dog around the house and a new baby arrives it is better to get rid of the dog. A jealous dog may attack the baby.

"If a dog arrives at a house after the baby, there is no danger. Dogs love children. But, when a mother pets her baby in the dog's presence, she should also pet the dog because the dog senses favoritism."

He depends on his wife to do most of his reading. They see plays together and go to the movies occasionally. If there is any action on stage or screen which requires explanation she whispers to him. Now that her own vision is as good as ever he is happy again—as happy, that is, as a James Thurber, sensitive and frequently disturbed by goings-on, can reasonably be expected to be.

At 58 he looks forward to a great deal more work. He may even go back to drawing, sitting on the back porch at West Cornwall with the south light over his shoulder, and a large black sheet ready for his white grease pencil.

Although Mr. Thurber and the *New Yorker* are inseparably linked in the minds of most people, the rapprochement was balked for a long time.

Mr. Thurber submitted between 30 and 40 stories and every story came back with dismaying promptness until he was persuaded that he was spending too much time on the stories.

He set himself a time limit, fixed an alarm clock to go off, and sat down and wrote about a man caught in a revolving door. He finished the story before the alarm sounded, sent off the manuscript, and it was accepted.

Mr. Ross hired him as managing editor, apparently thinking Mr.

Thurber was a friend of Mr. White's. Mr. Thurber and Mr. White actually had met only casually at a party once. Mr. Thurber didn't know he was managing editor until he was asked by a secretary to sign a payroll. He bridled, but Mr. Ross pointed out to him that writers were plentiful and editors scarce.

Mr. Thurber could write for the magazine, Mr. Ross agreed, but he would not get paid. Mr. Thurber wrote and wrote and wrote, and eventually was relieved of the managing editorship. For years he and Mr. White wrote "Talk of the Town" and rewrote articles. With Mr. Ross they set the tone of the magazine.

James Thurber: His Imagination Won Him Award

Marian Robb/1957

From *The Bermuda Mid-Ocean News*, April 26, 1957.
Reprinted with permission of Marian Robb and The Bermuda
Press (Holdings) Limited, publishers of *The Royal Gazette* and
The Bermuda Mid-Ocean News.

Humorist James Thurber, in between stints of working on his new
play with a Bermuda setting, has been basking in the island sun—
and also, for the past week, in the satisfaction of winning a new and
different literary award.

He is the first recipient, in the field of imaginative writing, of a
Liberty and Justice Book Award from the American Library Association.

The awards, initiated this year, go to authors of three books published in the previous year which "make distinguished contributions
to the American tradition of liberty and justice."

The winning writer in each field receives $5,000, provided by a
grant to the Library Association from the Fund for the Republic—a
special division of the Ford Foundation set up to encourage projects
in furtherance of civil rights and social justice.

The awards for 1956 were presented last night in New York. Mr.
Thurber received his in absentia, not feeling quite up to a quick flight
from Bermuda which would break his annual sojourn here. But he
sent along a speech of acceptance to be read for him. Like all his
writings, it was brief and to the point.

Noting that the humorous writer "expects to have his work taken as
fun, his connections as comic devices, and his deeper emotions as
thyroid imbalance," he said he received the honor with "a profound
and special pride."

And he went on to observe that, "Recent shadows are receding
and bright areas widening in the land to which the ALA, the Ford
Foundation, the Fund for the Republic and all of those here tonight

are so devoted and dedicated. But, if I may stick in a moral here, the higher the light of freedom is held, the smaller the dark hiding places become."

The Thurber book published last year which drew the award was *Further Fables for Our Time*—a collection of the author's familiar piquant fantasies which he completed last year in Bermuda. (He has been coming to the Colony for 26 years, his wife for 21. They have stayed in several homes from Somerset to Paget, and this year a cottage at "The Ledgelets" is Thurber Country.)

Interviewed there yesterday, Mr. Thurber carried on with a theme from his acceptance speech. Asked if he ever preached in his stories, he replied, "Some of my Fables are quite savage. But people can read the most savage stories I write and not get the point. They just say, 'Oh, our gentle humorist.' "

His next book, *The Wonderful O*—to be published May 20—is "also about freedom." He does not think its subject-matter will be looked at askance as it might have been a few years ago, when the American air was thick with suspicion of non-conformity. "It seems about two decades ago," he reflected, "that we were in such a crazy Alice-in-Wonderland state of mind."

Of the American temper in general, this thoroughly American writer remarked, "Americans are the bravest people in war, and the most jittery in peacetime—I don't know why, but we are the jumpiest people then."

Of the world in general, he hasn't too much hope—so long as men are running it and are bent on blowing it up. Said the veteran illustrator of implacable Amazons and defenseless males: "I've shifted way over to the side of women against men."

"Since when?" I asked, blinking slightly.

"Since they have really turned out to be the creative sex. Man is the destructive one, the one that blows the holy bejesus out of the planet, blows up what women create. But nature will take care of that by making women stronger—they already live longer. Men will get so weak they won't be able to fly around the throw things. If we believe in the future of the world, women will have to take over—and the sooner the better for me."

Even Bermuda, he thinks, must often be regarded by aircraft pilots as just a tempting target. From a fairy Island in peacetime, the atomic era turns it into "a great practice ground. I always think that everyone up in a plane now is thinking the wrong thing when he looks down."

Mr. Thurber remembers a forecast of the atomic age which only amused him at the time. "In 1922 there was a professor at Ohio State University who said we'd probably manage to split the atom in twenty years. I thought, 'You're interested in tiny things, you fellows.' He only missed it by two years."

Publication of *The Wonderful O* next month will be followed in the fall by the debut of another, *Alarms and Diversions*. This, his first collected edition since 1945, will contain a 15-year sampling of his zany stores, with illustrations done up until six years ago, when failing vision put an end to his drawing. Now he has to write large—about 20 words to a page—and dictates most of his output to a secretary.

"I work out of my head. That's probably why I'll have three books out within 12 months. I never could have done it when I could see; then I usually published one every two years."

(The *New Yorker* is still printing drawings signed "Th" from his previous 300 or 400 contributions.)

But James Thurber's eye for the ridiculous, the pompous or the bigoted, continues keen as ever—and that is about as keen as a Toledo blade. The tall and easy-mannered gentleman with ruddy face and thick sheaf of frosty hair has a mind like a dragon-fly—darting, probing, hovering and diving, poised on shimmering wings above some murky depth or weaving impromptu patterns in the startled air. No subject it attacks is ever quite the same again.

Yesterday his attention lingered for some time on Loch Ness—a story subject that took about two years to work up. The *Daily Mail* gave him all its clippings of stories on the monster, written over 24 years. They took ten hours just to read.

"The animal in the loch is now 24 years old," he said. "It's been seen 300 times by more than a thousand people, including a schoolmaster and a policeman this year. But a tremendous number of people try to delude themselves that there's nothing out there. One man wrote me that he had seen it for 30 seconds, but he was sure it was a hallucination."

He added that Loch Ness is about the size of Bermuda, and its monster is 40 feet long, makes 20 knots an hour, and is "timid and undangerous—it dives if you get very close."

This reminded him that he once wrote a story on "Extinct Animals of Bermuda." "I made them up, but many people took it seriously." Another pitfall of the literary jester.

Apropos of something that escapes me, Mr. Thurber voiced the view that American writers and artists die young, whereas their English counterparts live practically forever. "There is Phillpotts, writing for television at 94, and Laurence Housman still writing at 92."

The current play? Its title is *Welcoming Arms*. It is set in front of a Bermuda house, "Serenity Hall," to which Americans have fled for peace and quiet. Instead, the author confided, "All hell breaks loose. It's an Enoch Arden story." Elliott Nugent will be co-producer and play a leading role.

Before it is ready for Broadway, designers will have to come to Bermuda to see how to make authentic sets. For one thing, they must record the night song of the tree-toads.

A Sunday Afternoon with Mr. Thurber

Maurice Dolbier/1957

From *The Herald Tribune* Book Review, November 2, 1957, p. 2.
I.H.T. Corporation. Reprinted by permission.

"That room in there," said James Thurber. "I call it the Ghost Room. Broun and Benchley and Woollcott and Ross and all the rest. Still, I suppose no ghost really haunts the Algonquin. There'd be too much competition.

"I'm calling my next book, *The Years with Ross.*" (The first of six selections from the book is published in the current Jubilee issue of The *Atlantic Monthly.*) "There were almost twenty-five of them. From February, 1927 to December, 1951. Every one who knew Ross is giving me the finest kind of assistance. I've been given the use of a *New Yorker* office and the services of a *New Yorker* secretary, even though I'm writing the articles for another magazine. The Ross correspondence has been made available to me, some 30,000 letters, and Ross stands there on every page. Yet, as Andy White says, 'The more light that's thrown on Ross, the more mysterious he becomes.' My secretary stops every now and then while I'm dictating and says, 'Are you sure you're not making this up?' I'm not. I couldn't. No one's imagination could be that robust.

"When I was in France in 1926, writing for the *Chicago Tribune,* I received a check from *Harper's* 'The Lion's Mouth' for a piece on 'The Street Fights of Paris.' It came to 3,600 francs, and was just in time. I owed money at my Left Bank hotel, and I'd borrowed money on my return ticket to the United States. When I came back to this country, I had $10 left. I borrowed another twenty from a girl I'd met in passing at Nice. I lived in one room on 13th St., and sent stuff to the *New Yorker*, which was rejected. I wrote a book of parody called *Why We Behave Like Microbe Hunters* that every one turned down—the *New Yorker, Harper's, Holt, John Farrar.* The sales departments were the bottlenecks. They said it was hard enough trying to sell a first novel. A first book of humor was impossible. Later

45

Harper's and the *New Yorker* used it anyway, without knowing it. I'd rewritten it.

"Then I took a job on the *New York Post* as a reporter. The staff included Nunnally Johnson, Laura Hobson, Russell Crouse, Forrest Davis, Bruce Gould and Norman Klein, who wrote one of the best mystery novels I've ever read, *No, No, the Woman.* Later Crouse moved to the *New Yorker.* So did I.

"When I write, I rewrite five or ten times all along the way. It's different with drawing. I spoil my drawings if I do them more than once. Andy White found me doing some cross-hatching on a drawing one day and said, 'Stop! If you ever become good, you'll be mediocre.' I stopped.

"I have about six different things under way now. There's a play about Harold Ross that I started in 1945, and plan to finish later, hoping that the play will benefit by the book. I'm working on three book-length fairy stories. And there's 'The Train on Track 5.' No, it's not a novel. I haven't written a novel, and don't plan to. It seems today that after youngsters get over the braces on their teeth, and then get through college, the next thing you hear their mother saying is, 'Thank God, Tom or Harry has gotten over his first novel.'

"No, 'The Train on Track 5'* is a satire on modern American life, done in terms of fairy tale and dream. I've been working on it, off and on, for some time, and it hasn't quite come right yet. My wife read a part of it aloud to some of our friends. I asked how it was received, and she said, 'Well, some one kept making ugly sounds with their lips all through the reading. Me.' Helen is one of the greatest proofreaders, editors, and critics I've ever known. She's often rescued things I've thrown aside. And, if there's something she doesn't like, she pulls no punches. When I wrote "The Secret Life of Walter Mitty," I had a scene in which Mitty got between Hemingway and an opponent in a Stork Club brawl. Helen said that had to come out, that there should be nothing topical in the story. Well, you know how it is when your wife is right. You grouse around the house for a week, and then you follow her advice.

"An author's best book is always the one he hasn't done yet and isn't quite sure he can do. Some one once said, 'The thing is to last

*Thurber worked on this project extensively, but never completed it.—TF

and to get your work done.' That's horrible. What in the name of God can a man do if his work is done? The English write into their 80's and 90's, most Americans seem to stop (or be stopped) around 57. Mencken told me he'd done more work in the ten years between 58 and 68 than in any comparable period during his life. I'll be 63 in December, and *Alarms and Diversions* (Harper) will be my third book in twelve months.

"A blind man benefits by a lack of distractions. I remember sitting with Ross at a table in this restaurant. He picked up a bottle of Worchestershire sauce and then threw it down, saying, 'Goddamit, that's the 10,000th time I've read the label on this bottle.' I told him, 'Goddamit, Harold, that's because you're handicapped by vision.'

"The luckiest thing that can happen to a blind man is to have total recall. I first found out I had it in 1913, when I was in a psychology class at Ohio State. There were forty in the class, conducted by a Viennese professor named Weiss. He read a 1,000-word piece to us, and then told us to write down as much as we could remember. My score was 78 per cent, the next highest was 20. Three weeks later, he told us to write down as much as we could remember. This time my score was 50 per cent, the next highest was 6. My mother had total recall, too. She could remember the birthday of a girl I was in love with in the third grade. So can I. Oct. 9.

"I seem to have acquired the reputation of being anti-Woman. But for every 100 letters I get, 95 are from women, and they're generally friendly. It's the men who write things like 'What makes you think you're so funny?' A Congressman once told me he'd been asked why Thurber hadn't been investigated. He said, 'There are two reasons. First, we're afraid of him. And, second, our wives and daughters wouldn't stand for it.' "

"Call Me Jim": James Thurber Speaking

Eddy Gilmore/1958

From *The Columbus Sunday Dispatch*, August 3, 1958, Society sec., pp. 20, 21. Reprinted with permission of The Associated Press.

LONDON, AUG. 2—(AP)—James Thurber, who is perhaps the world's greatest living humorist, isn't quite sure he's funny.

Take the case of the seal in the bedroom, that mad drawing of a sea beast sublimely clinging to the head board of a married couple's bed.

"It was all an accident," said Thurber a little sadly.

"The first drawing was of a seal on a rock and he was looking at two dots in the distance and the caption was, 'Hmm, explorers.' "

Thurber knew that wasn't very funny.

In trying to do it over again, the rock turned itself into the head of a bed. And beneath the precariously perched seal appeared a man and a woman halfway between the sheets.

"All right, have it your way," said the woman irately to her husband. "You heard a seal bark."

In that crazy juxtaposition of animal, man, bed and woman and the wildly illogical logic of this bedroom scene, Thurber made millions of people laugh.

After the drawing and caption were published in the *New Yorker* magazine, Thurber received a telegram from the late Robert Benchley thanking him for the "funniest line drawing" ever to appear in a magazine.

"I thought to myself," explained Thurber, " 'What's he talking about?' "

Early this summer Thurber came to London to get some peace and quiet, but it's been one long interruption ever since.

Most of the distractions have been from the British press, television and radio. Also from a few Americans, Scandinavians, Germans, Netherlanders, Greeks and Latins. No Russians though.

Oddly, he doesn't seem to mind.

48

On few subjects is the British press more anti-American than on Thurber.

The anti-Americanism manifests itself in a strange way, for in their unashamed hero worship of this tall, gangling, gentle native of Columbus, Ohio, the British fiercely resent his being American.

Since arriving, Thurber's opinions have been assiduously solicited by press, TV and radio on everything from the future of humor in the nuclear age to the sex life of frustrated bloodhounds.

"I'm getting tired of hearing about myself over here," he said. But he said it softly. And almost as if he felt he was to blame for getting tired of himself.

At 63 he is blind.

"I don't see anything at all except light—even in the darkest room," he explained. "Soft diffusion of light without figures or landscape."

Perhaps this in some way has something to do with the magic of his conversation, for listening to James Thurber is a rare and wonderful experience.

His words come out like a torrent of bright and lively fragments in a kaleidoscope. But, sit back and listen and there's sense and even pattern in their profusion.

Thurber is an easy talker, but like the kaleidoscope, he performs best if you jiggle him every few minutes.

"Did you ever own a dog, Mr. Thurber?"

"Dogs! I've owned 70 dogs since I was a boy. Dogs have a sense of humor. And in the first place a French Poodle. They don't use them as police dogs and that's not because they are too dumb, but because they are too smart . . . I played a joke on my dog once. He didn't particularly like it. You know, you can carry a joke against a dog too far. For three days my dog wouldn't shake hands . . . I don't think I've ever drawn a goat. I've drawn all kinds of dangerous beasts including the human male . . . "

"Women, Mr. Thurber?"

"People ask me if I hate women because of my drawings of them. I couldn't draw a pretty woman . . . I once had a drawing in which one of the women should have been pretty. I suggested to Ross (the late Harold Ross, editor of the New Yorker) that I draw four of the women and he get some other artist to draw the pretty woman. But

Ross wouldn't agree. He said there would be trouble trying to work out the payment. I told him there wouldn't be any trouble at all. I said, 'I'm drawing four women and this other fellow's drawing one woman. Just pay me four-fifths of the money and give him the other fifth,'" but he wouldn't do it.

"Women, h-mm. When I get mad at women it's usually because they fall behind my standard . . . when my daughter was born they told me that she was three inches longer than any other girl child born in that hospital for the last five years. I said to myself, 'Yes, Thurber, you're the spearhead father of the new dominant sex.' Then I began to develop the idea that since the American woman was getting bigger all the time, this was just nature's plan to preserve our species—since the male is destroying it . . . "

"You used to be a newspaper man, Mr. Thurber?"

"Yes, but don't call me Mr. Thurber. Call me Jim. I was working in New York once and the fellow who was running the paper decided one day that all the leads of all the stories should consist of one word. You know, one-word leads.

"Well, I wrote one one day that began—'Dead.' That was the one-word lead and the second paragraph said, 'That was what the man was the police found in an area-way last night.' Well, he didn't like that very much but he kept on with the one-word leads until one night when he said to me, 'Thurber, there's a real sexy play over at the such and such theater. Go over there and write a story about it.'

"I came back and my one-word lead was a word that neither my paper—nor your paper—would publish. I wrote that word down and then my second paragraph said—'That was the word flung across the footlights yesterday.' 'All right. All right,' said the boss, 'Thurber and everybody else are starting to kid the hell out of it, so we'll go back to leads that make sense.'

"My Drawing? I've never taken it very seriously. I can't draw anymore at all. I tried it with a luminous pencil when I was getting real blind. But even this didn't work . . .

"My blindness? When someone doesn't bring up the subject I usually do . . . when you're blind you naturally take a great interest in eyes. I want to write about the human eye, because it occurs to me that the human being knows less about it than any other part of the body. He considers it a delicate organ. It's the toughest thing in the body. Those eyedrops, why if you take them internally they'd make you spit cotton for a month.

"The eye is the one part of the body that is the same size at birth as in maturity. That's why all babies are beautiful. Old Rube Goldberg answered the question, what becomes of all the beautiful babies? 'Their heads get bigger,' he said. 'Their eyes don't.'

"I like to look straight at the person I'm talking to. It makes them feel better. Of course, my wife Helen has to yell at me if they get up and go away, as they are sometimes likely to do when I'm telling a real good story. You feel kind of foolish talking to an empty room . . . Even Helen isn't always too helpful. I got to the end of telling her a great story one day. I expected at least a laugh. She'd gone into the bathroom, though, and all I got was the familiar domestic gurgle of running water . . .

"In blindness this total recall that I have helps me greatly. It stands me in good stead, this trick memory. I knew I had it as far back as 1913 when a professor came into the room one day and read us several pages of something and then asked us to write down what we could remember of it . . . I remembered 84 per cent and three weeks later I could recall 50 per cent of it.

"Total recall is a strange thing. It doesn't seem so much to please you that you have it—but that others don't . . . I can remember hundreds of telephone numbers, some of them going back as far as 1907 . . . I could visualize pages of a whole book after I'd read it.

"My process of going blind was very slow, so I got very well adjusted to it. The hardest thing to learn for me is to dictate. I've been a typewriter man all my life. After I went totally blind I wrote by hand in the morning . . . "

Now that he is blind and those wonderful drawings are gone, more and more of their wild magic is getting into the speculating splendor of his writing, a lot of which he is going to do in London.

"I can get a lot done here," he said, "I don't know what it is unless the page is different. See here, when you're being interviewed in New York, you sit on the end of your chair. Here, you lean back."

Writers at Work: James Thurber

George Plimpton and Max Steele/1958

The Hôtel Continental, just down from the Place Ven-
dôme on the Rue Castiglione. It is from here that Janet
Flanner (Genêt) sends her Paris letter to *The New Yorker,*
and it is here that the Thurbers usually stay while in Paris.
"We like it because the service is first-rate without being
snobbish."

Thurber was standing to greet us in a small salon whose
cold European formality had been somewhat softened
and warmed by well-placed vases of flowers, stacks and
portable shelves of American novels in bright dust jackets,
and by pads of yellow paper and bouquets of yellow
pencils on the desk. Thurber impresses one immediately
by his physical size. After years of delighting in the shy,
trapped little man in the Thurber cartoons and the con-
fused and bewildered man who has fumbled in and out of
some of the funniest books written in this century, we,
perhaps like many readers, were expecting to find the
frightened little man in person. Not at all. Thurber by his
firm handgrasp and confident voice and the way he
lowered himself into his chair gave the impression of out-
ward calmness and assurance. Though his eyesight has
almost failed him, it is not a disability which one is aware of
for more than the opening minute, and if Thurber seems to
be the most nervous person in the room, it is because he
has learned to put his visitors so completely at ease.

He talks in a surprisingly boyish voice, which is flat with
the accents of the Midwest where he was raised and,
though slow in tempo, never dull. He is not an easy man to
pin down with questions. He prefers to sidestep them and,
rather than instructing, he entertains with a vivid series of
anecdotes and reminiscences.

Opening the interview with a long history of the bloodhound, Thurber was only with some difficulty persuaded
to shift to a discussion of his craft. Here again his manner
was typical—the anecdotes, the reminiscences punctu-
ated with direct quotes and factual data. His powers of
memory are astounding. In quoting anyone—perhaps a
conversation of a dozen years before—Thurber pauses
slightly, his voice changes in tone, and you know what
you're hearing is exactly as it was said.

Thurber: Well, you know it's a nuisance—to have memory like
mine—as well as an advantage. It's . . . well . . . like a whore's top
drawer. There's so much else in there that's junk—costume jewelry,
unnecessary telephone numbers whose exchanges no longer exist.
For instance, I can remember the birthday of anybody who's ever
told me his birthday. Dorothy Parker—August 22, Lewis Gannett—
October 3, Andy White—July 9, Mrs. White—September 17. I can
go on with about two hundred. So can my mother. She can tell you
the birthday of the girl I was in love with in the third grade, in 1903.
Offhand, just like that. I got my powers of memory from her. Sometimes it helps out in the most extraordinary way. You remember
Robert M. Coates? Bob Coates? He is the author of *The Eater of
Darkness,* which Ford Madox Ford called the first true Dadaist novel.
Well, the week after Stephen Vincent Benét died—Coates and I had
both known him—we were talking about Benét. Coates was trying to
remember an argument he had had with Benét some fifteen years
before. He couldn't remember. I said, "I can." Coates told me that
was impossible since I hadn't been there. "Well," I said, "you happened to mention it in passing about twelve years ago. You were
arguing about a play called *Swords.*" I was right, and Coates was
able to take it up from there. But it's strange to reach a position
where your friends have to be supplied with their own memories. It's
bad enough dealing with your own.
  Interviewers: Still, it must be a great advantage for the writer. I
don't suppose you have to take notes.
  Thurber: No. I don't have to do the sort of thing Fitzgerald did
with *The Last Tycoon*—the voluminous, the tiny and meticulous

notes, the long descriptions of character. I can keep all these things in
my mind. I wouldn't have to write down "three roses in a vase" or
something, or a man's middle name. Henry James dictated notes just
the way that I write. His note writing was part of the creative act,
which is why his prefaces are so good. He dictated notes to see what
it was they might come to.

Interviewers: Then you don't spend much time prefiguring your
work?

Thurber: No. I don't bother with charts and so forth. Elliott
Nugent, on the other hand, is a careful constructor. When we were
working on *The Male Animal* together, he was constantly concerned
with plotting the play. He could plot the thing from back to front—
what was going to happen here, what sort of situation would end the
first-act, curtain, and so forth. I can't work that way. Nugent would
say, "Well, Thurber, we've got our problem, we've got all these people in the living room. Now what are we going to do with them?" I'd
say that I didn't know and couldn't tell him until I'd sat down at the
typewriter and found out. I don't believe the writer should know too
much where he's going. If he does, he runs into old man blueprint—
old man propaganda.

Interviewers: Is the act of writing easy for you?

Thurber: For me it's mostly a question of rewriting. It's part of a
constant attempt on my part to make the finished version smooth, to
make it seem effortless. A story I've been working on—"The Train on
Track Six," it's called—was rewritten fifteen complete times. There
must have been close to 240,000 words in all the manuscripts put
together, and I must have spent two thousand hours working at it. Yet
the finished version can't be more than twenty thousand words.

Interviewers: Then it's rare that your work comes out right the
first time?

Thurber: Well, my wife took a look at the first version of something I was doing not long ago and said, "Goddamn it, Thurber,
that's high-school stuff." I have to tell her to wait until the seventh
draft, it'll work out all right. I don't know why that should be so, that
the first or second draft of everything I write reads as if it was turned
out by a charwoman. I've only written one piece quickly. I wrote a
thing called "File and Forget" in one afternoon—but only because it
was a series of letters just as one would ordinarily dictate. And I'd

have to admit that the last letter of the series, after doing all the others that one afternoon, took me a week. It was the end of the pieces and I had to fuss over it.

Interviewers: Does the fact that you're dealing with humor slow down the production?

Thurber: It's possible. With humor you have to look out for traps. You're likely to be very gleeful with what you've first put down, and you think it's fine, very funny. One reason you go over and over it is to make the piece sound less as if you were having a lot of fun with it yourself. You try to play it down. In fact, if there's such a thing as a *New Yorker* style, that would be it—playing it down.

Interviewers: Do you envy those who write at high speed, as against your method of constant revision?

Thurber: Oh, no, I don't, though I do admire their luck. Hervey Allen, you know, the author of the big best-seller *Anthony Adverse,* seriously told a friend of mine who was working on a biographical piece on Allen that he could close his eyes, lie down on a bed, and hear the voices of his ancestors. Furthermore there was some sort of angel-like creature that danced along his pen while he was writing. He wasn't balmy by any means. He just felt he was in communication with some sort of metaphysical recorder. So you see the novelists have all the luck. I never knew a humorist who got any help from his ancestors. Still, the act of writing is either something the writer dreads or actually likes, and I actually like it. Even rewriting's fun. You're getting somewhere, whether it seems to move or not. I remember Elliot Paul and I used to argue about rewriting back in 1925 when we both worked for the *Chicago Tribune* in Paris. It was his conviction you should leave the story as it came out of the typewriter, no changes. Naturally, he worked fast. Three novels he could turn out, each written in three week's time. I remember once he came into the office and said that a sixty-thousand-word manuscript had been stolen. No carbons existed, no notes. We were all horrified. But it didn't bother him at all. He'd just get back to the typewriter and bat away again. But for me—writing as fast as that would seem too facile. Like my drawings, which I do very quickly, sometimes so quickly that the result is an accident, something I hadn't intended at all. People in the arts I've run into in France are constantly indignant when I say I'm a writer and not an artist. They tell me I mustn't run down my drawings. I try to explain that I do them for relaxation, and that I do them too fast for them to be called art.

Interviewers: You say that your drawings often don't come out the way you intended?

Thurber: Well, once I did a drawing for *The New Yorker* of a naked woman on all fours up on top of a bookcase—a big bookcase. She's up there near the ceiling, and in the room are her husband and two other women. The husband is saying to one of the women, obviously a guest, "This is the present Mrs. Harris. That's my first wife up there." Well, when I did the cartoon originally I meant the naked woman to be at the top of a flight of stairs, but I lost the sense of perspective and instead of getting in the stairs when I drew my line down, there she was stuck up there, naked, on a bookcase.

Incidentally, that cartoon really threw *The New Yorker* editor, Harold Ross. He approached any humorous piece of writing, or more particularly a drawing, not only grimly but realistically. He called me on the phone and asked if the woman on the bookcase was supposed to be alive, stuffed, or dead. I said, "I don't know, but I'll let you know in a couple of hours." After a while I called him back and told him I'd just talked to my taxidermist, who said you can't stuff a woman, that my doctor had told me a dead woman couldn't support herself on all fours. "So, Ross," I said, "she must be alive." "Well, then," he said, "what's she doing up there naked in the home of her husband's second wife?" I told him he had me there.

Interviewers: But he published it.

Thurber: Yes, he published it, growling a bit. He had a fine understanding of humor, Ross, though he couldn't have told you about it. When I introduced Ross to the work of Peter de Vries, he first said, "He won't be good; he won't be funny; he won't know English." (He was the only successful editor I've known who approached everything like a ship going on the rocks.) But when Ross had looked at the work he said, "How can you get this guy on the phone?" He couldn't have said why, but he had that bloodhound instinct. The same with editing. He was a wonderful man at detecting something wrong with a story without knowing why.

Interviewers: Could he develop a writer?

Thurber: Not really. It wasn't true what they often said of him—that he broke up writers like matches—but still he wasn't the man to

develop a writer. He was an unread man. Well, he'd read Mark
Twain's *Life on the Mississippi* and several other books he told me
about—medical books—and he took the Encyclopedia Britannica to
the bathroom with him. I think he was about up to H when he died.
But still his effect on writers was considerable. When you first met
him you couldn't believe he was the editor of *The New Yorker* and
afterward you couldn't believe that anyone else could have been.
The main thing he was interested in was clarity. Someone once said
of *The New Yorker* that it never contained a sentence that would
puzzle an intelligent fourteen-year-old or in any way affect her morals
badly. Ross didn't like that, but nevertheless he was a purist and
perfectionist and it had a tremendous effect on all of us: it kept us
from being sloppy. When I first met him he asked me if I knew
English. I thought he meant French or a foreign language. But he
repeated, "Do you know English?" When I said I did he replied,
"Goddamn it, nobody knows English." As Andy White mentioned in
his obituary, Ross approached the English sentence as though it was
an enemy, something that was going to throw him. He used to fuss
for an hour over a comma. He'd call me in for lengthy discussions
about the Thurber colon. And as for poetic license, he'd say, "Damn
any license to get things wrong." In fact, Ross read so carefully that
often he didn't get the sense of your story. I once said: "I wish you'd
read my stories for pleasure, Ross." He replied he hadn't time for
that.

Interviewers: It's strange that one of the main ingredients of
humor—low comedy—has never been accepted for *The New Yorker.*

Thurber: Ross had a neighbor woman's attitude about it. He
never got over his Midwestern provincialism. His idea was that sex is
an incident. "If you can prove it," I said, "we can get it in a box on
the front pages of *The New York Times.*" Now I don't want to say
that in private life Ross was a prude. But as regards the theater or the
printed page he certainly was. For example, he once sent an office
memorandum to us in a sealed envelope. It was an order: "When
you send me a memorandum with four-letter words in it, *seal it.*
There are women in this office." I said, "Yah, Ross, and they know a
lot more of these words than you do." When women were around he
was very conscious of them. Once my wife and I were in his office
and Ross was discussing a man and woman he knew much better

than we did. Ross told us, "I have *every* reason to believe that they're s-L-E-E-P-I-N-G together." My wife replied, "Why, Harold Ross, what words you do spell out." But honest to goodness, that was genuine. Women are either good or bad, he once told me, and the good ones must not hear these things.

Incidentally, I'm telling these things to refresh my memory. I'm doing a short book on him called "Ross in Charcoal." I'm putting a lot of this stuff in. People may object, but after all it's a portrait of the man and I see no reason for not putting it in.

Interviewers: Did he have much direct influence on your own work?

Thurber: After the seven years I spent in newspaper writing, it was more E. B. White who taught me about writing, how to clear up sloppy journalese. He was a strong influence, and for a long time in the beginning I thought he might be too much of one. But at least he got me away from a rather curious style I was starting to perfect—tight journalese laced with heavy doses of Henry James.

Interviewers: But there were things to be learned from him?

Thurber: Yes, but again he was an influence you had to get over. Especially if you wrote for *The New Yorker.* Harold Ross wouldn't have understood it. I once wrote a piece called "The Beast in the Dingle" which everybody took as a parody. Actually it was a conscious attempt to write the story as James would have written it. Ross looked at it and said: "Goddamn it, this is too literary; I got only fifteen per cent of the allusions." My wife and I often tried to figure out which were the fifteen per cent he could have got.

You know, I've occasionally wondered what James would have done with our world. I've just written a piece—"Preface to Old Friends," it's called—in which James at the age of a hundred and four writes a preface to a novel about our age in which he summarizes the trends and complications, but at the end is so completely lost he doesn't really care enough to read it over to find his way out again.

That's the trouble with James. You get bored with him finally. He lived in the time of four-wheelers, and no bombs, and the problems then seemed a bit special and separate. That's one reason you feel restless reading him. James is like—well, I had a bulldog once who used to drag rails around, enormous ones—six-, eight-, twelve-foot rails. He loved to get them in the middle and you'd hear him growling out there, trying to bring the thing home. Once he brought home a chest of drawers—without the drawers in it. Found it on an ashheap. Well, he'd start to get these things in the garden gate, everything finely balanced, you see, and then *crash,* he'd come up against the gate posts. He'd get it through finally, but I had that feeling in some of the James novels: that he was trying to get that rail through a gate not wide enough for it.

Interviewers: How about Mark Twain? Pretty much everybody believes him to have been the major influence on American humorists.

Thurber: Everybody wants to know if I've learned from Mark Twain. Actually I've never read much of him. I did buy *Tom Sawyer,* but dammit, I'm sorry, I've not got around to reading it all the way through. I told H. L. Mencken that, and he was shocked. He said America had produced only two fine novels: *Huck Finn* and *Babbitt.* Of course it's always a matter of personal opinion—these lists of the great novels. I can remember calling Frank Harris—he was about seventy then—when I was on the *Chicago Tribune's* edition in Nice. In his house he had three portraits on the wall—Mark Twain, Frank Harris, and I think it was Hawthorne. Harris was in the middle. Harris would point up to them and say, "Those three are the best American writers. The one in the middle is the best." Harris really thought he was wonderful. Once he told me he was going to live to be a hundred. When I asked him what the formula was, he told me it was very simple. He said, "I've bought myself a stomach pump and one half-hour after dinner I pump myself out." Can you imagine that? Well, it didn't work. It's a wonder it didn't kill him sooner.

Interviewers: Could we ask you why you've never attempted a long work?

Thurber: I've never wanted to write a long work. Many writers feel a sense of frustration or something if they haven't, but I don't.

Interviewers: Perhaps the fact that you're writing humor imposes a limit on the length of a work.

Thurber: Possibly. But brevity in any case—whether the work is supposed to be humorous or not—would seem to me to be desirable. Most of the books I like are short books: *The Red Badge of Courage, The Turn of the Screw,* Conrad's short stories, *A Lost Lady,*

Joseph Hergesheimer's *Wild Oranges,* Victoria Lincoln's *February Hill, The Great Gatsby* . . . . .You know Fitzgerald once wrote Thomas Wolfe: "You're a putter-inner and I'm a taker-outer." I stick with Fitzgerald. I don't believe, as Wolfe did, that you have to turn out a massive work before being judged a writer. Wolfe once told me at a cocktail party I didn't know what it was to be a writer. My wife, standing next to me, complained about that. "But my husband *is* a writer," she said. Wolfe was genuinely surprised. "He is?" he asked. "Why, all I ever see is that stuff of his in *The New Yorker.*" In other words, he felt that prose under five thousand words was certainly not the work of a writer . . . it was some kind of doodling in words. If you said you were a writer, he wanted to know where the books were, the great big long books. He was really genuine about that.

I was interested to see William Faulkner's list not so long ago of the five most important American authors of this century. According to him Wolfe was first, Faulkner second—let's see, now that Wolfe's dead that puts Faulkner up there in the lead, doesn't it? — Dos Passos third, then Hemingway, and finally Steinbeck. It's interesting that the first three are putter-inners. They write expansive novels.

Interviewers: Wasn't Faulkner's criterion whether or not the author dared to go out on a limb?

Thurber: It seems to me you're going out on a limb these days to keep a book short.

Interviewers: Though you've never done a long serious work you have written stories—"The Cane in the Corridor" and "The Whippoorwill" in particular—in which the mood is far from humorous.

Thurber: In anything funny you write that isn't close to serious you've missed something along the line. But in those stories of which you speak there was an element of anger—something I wanted to get off my chest. I wrote "The Whippoorwill" after five eye operations. It came somewhere out of a grim fear in the back of my mind. I've never been able to trace it.

Interviewers: Some critics think that much of your work can be traced to the depicting of trivia as a basis for humor. In fact, there's been some criticism—

Thurber: Which is trivia—the diamond or the elephant? Any humorist must be interested in trivia, in every little thing that occurs in a household. It's what Robert Benchley did so well—in fact so well that one of the greatest fears of the humorous writer is that he has spent three weeks writing something done faster and better by Benchley in 1919. Incidentally, you never got very far talking to Benchley about humor. He'd do a take-off of Max Eastman's *Enjoyment of Laughter.* "We must understand," he'd say, "that all sentences which begin with W are funny."

Interviewers: Would you care to define humor in terms of your own work?

Thurber: Well, someone once wrote a definition of the difference between English and American humor. I wish I could remember his name. I thought his definition very good. He said that the English treat the commonplace as if it were remarkable and the Americans treat the remarkable as if it were commonplace. I believe that's true of humorous writing. Years ago we did a parody of *Punch* in which Benchley did a short piece depicting a wife bursting into a room and shouting "The primroses are in bloom!"—treating the commonplace as remarkable, you see. In "The Secret Life of Walter Mitty" I tried to treat the remarkable as commonplace.

Interviewers: Does it bother you to talk about the stories on which you're working? It bothers many writers, though it would seem that particularly the humorous story is polished through retelling.

Thurber: Oh, yes. I often tell them at parties and places. And I write them there too.

Interviewers: You write them?

Thurber: I never quite know when I'm not writing. Sometimes my wife comes up to me at a party and says, "Dammit, Thurber, stop writing." She usually catches me in the middle of a paragraph. Or my daughter will look up from the dinner table and ask, "Is he sick?" "No," my wife says, "he's writing something." I have to do it that way on account of my eyes. I still write occasionally—in the proper sense of the word—using black crayon on yellow paper and getting perhaps twenty words to the page. My usual method, though, is to spend the mornings turning over the text in my mind. Then in the afternoon, between two and five, I call in a secretary and dictate to her. I can do about two thousand words. It took me about ten years to learn.

Interviewers: How about the new crop of writers? Do you note any good humorists coming along with them?

Thurber: There don't seem to be many coming up. I once had a psychoanalyst tell me that the depression had a considerable effect—much worse than Hitler and the war. It's a tradition for a child to see his father in uniform as something glamorous—not his father coming home from Wall Street in a three-button sack suit saying, "We're ruined," and the mother bursting into tears—a catastrophe that to a child's mind is unexplainable. There's been a great change since the thirties. In those days students used to ask me what Peter Arno did at night. And about Dorothy Parker. Now they want to know what my artistic credo is. An element of interest seems to have gone out of them.

Interviewers: Has the shift in the mood of the times had any effect on your own work?

Thurber: Well, *The Thurber Album* was written at a time when in America there was a feeling of fear and suspicion. It's quite different from *My Life and Hard Times,* which was written earlier and is a funnier and better book. The *Album* was kind of an escape—going back to the Middle West of the last century and the beginning of this, when there wasn't this fear and hysteria. I wanted to write the story of some solid American characters, more or less as an example of how Americans started out and what they should go back to—to sanity and soundness and away from this jumpiness. It's hard to write humor in the mental weather we've had, and that's likely to take you into reminiscence. Your heart isn't in it to write anything funny. In the years 1950 to 1953 I did very few things, nor did they appear in *The New Yorker.* Now, actually, I think the situation is beginning to change for the better.

Interviewers: No matter what the "mental climate," though, you would continue writing?

Thurber: Well, the characteristic fear of the American writer is not so much that as it is the process of aging. The writer looks in the mirror and examines his hair and teeth to see if they're still with him. "Oh my God," he says, "I wonder how my writing is. I bet I can't write today." The only time I met Faulkner he told me he wanted to live long enough to do three more novels. He was fifty-three then, and I think he *has* done them. Then Hemingway says, you know, that he doesn't expect to be alive after sixty. But he doesn't look forward *not* to being. When I met Hemingway with John O'Hara in

Costello's Bar five or six years ago we sat around and talked about how *old* we were getting. You see it's constantly on the minds of American writers. I've never known a woman who could weep about her age the way the men I know can.

Coupled with this fear of aging is the curious idea that the writer's inventiveness and ability will end in his fifties. And of course it often does. Carl van Vechten stopped writing. The prolific Joseph Herge-sheimer suddenly couldn't write any more. Over here in Europe that's never been the case—Hardy, for instance, who started late and kept going. Of course Keats had good reason to write, "When I have fears that I may cease to be Before my pen has glean'd my teeming brain." That's the great classic statement. But in America the writer is more likely to fear that his brain may cease to teem. I once did a drawing of a man at his typewriter, you see, and all this crumpled paper is on the floor, and he's staring down in discouragement. "What's the matter," his wife is saying, "has your pen gleaned your teeming brain?"

Interviewers: In your case there wouldn't be much chance of this?

Thurber: No. I write basically because it's so much fun—even though I can't see. When I'm not writing, as my wife knows, I'm miserable. I don't have that fear that suddenly it will all stop. I have enough outlined to last me as long as I live.

James Thurber: "Humor Is a Gentle Thing"

Rod Nordell/1959

From *The Christian Science Monitor,* June 4, 1959, p. 11. Reprinted by permission from *The Christian Science Monitor.* © 1959 by The Christian Science Publishing Society. All rights reserved.

"Humor is a gentle thing. That's why it is so necessary if our species is to survive."

James Thurber speaking.

Unlike humorists who belittle efforts to discuss their art he says, "The more it's talked about the better."

He was talking about it at a time when any author might be expected to refuse callers—a few hours before a reception on the publication date of his new book (*The Years with Ross*).

This was going to be what a New York editor called the "literary party of the year." Mrs. Thurber was keeping her husband in his dressing gown, so he wouldn't have to dress twice on this hot New York day. But she had said on the phone to come on up to their rooms at the Algonquin.

The Thurbers' door stood hospitably open. Mr. Thurber rose and put out his hand. To a midwestern ear his voice had comforting midwestern traces. I recognized Mrs. Thurber as the woman I had seen in the lobby shortly before, chatting with the desk attendants and saying, as she entered the elevator. "I think I'll just give him a glass of cold milk."

"Don't think I always loaf around like this," Mr. Thurber said.

He sat near an air conditioner that was whirring softly in a window. A pretransistor portable radio was close by on a table. (Was it the portable he described in "Back Home Again"—"I don't know why I had taken it with me, since it doesn't work very well anywhere, at sea level or high up in the mountains of Virginia, or not so high in the foothills of the Berkshires"?) Mrs. Thurber worked at a desk, now and then adding a word to the conversation.

Humor does not thrive in days like these when we are bombarded by descriptions of disease and threats of destruction, Mr. Thurber said. Farce thrives, and fast musical comedy, but not "something carefully thought out."

A magazine had asked him to do an article on the current "humor of horror," but he had refused because to him it is not humor, just horror. "Humor must never be identified with horror."

But wasn't some of Mr. Thurber's own humor touched with the horror, "The Unicorn in the Garden," for example—or, Mrs. Thurber ventured, "The Whippoorwill"?

The point here is that he doesn't always write humor, Mr. Thurber explained. He tries to do some of everything. He mentioned that Dorothy Parker had called his work "serious comedy," which is not far from T. S. Eliot's description of it as "a form of humor which is also a way of saying something serious."

At the moment, Mr. Thurber is maintaining his variety by working on a "serious, sometimes savage" satire, "The Grawk": a long-promised play about the *New Yorker* based on *The Years with Ross*; and something or other involving the letter P.

Mr. Thurber has already published a book called *The Wonderful O,* but he said that he thinks P is the most fascinating letter of the alphabet—the letter of pixies like Peter Pan, Punch, Peg o' My Heart, and Pooh; of Ponce de León Percival, and Peary; of curious animals like the panda, penguin, poodle, ptarmigan, and pterodactyl. And he hasn't yet started on the possibilities of his OED (*Oxford English Dictionary*).

Somehow this part of the discussion reminded Mr. Thurber of a man who spoke of "the trivia I waste my time on." Well, everything can't be gloria mundi, Mr. Thurber said, we need a little trivia mundi, too. "A humorist can't take himself too seriously; he doesn't dare."

The word "grawk," which one of the bemused correspondents in Thurber's "Pet Department" thought was the voice of a raven ("I have never known a raven that said anything but "'Ark,'" the pet expert replied), is now a substitute for the word "spoodle," which Mr. Thurber rejected after being told it is a coinage for a dog part spaniel and part poodle. "The Grawk" deals with an "unidentified flying thing" that attacks the roofs of a city. Mr. Thurber is interested in what "politicians and presidents of garden clubs" might do in such circumstances. He is also interested in the possibility that if an object of fear is discovered to be simply nothing at all the authorities may try to create one.

Does Mr. Thurber think humor can have a reforming purpose?

"That was one of our big failures during the Dark Ages (Mr. Thurber's phrase for the period of McCarthyism). We used direct attack instead of ridicule." He quoted a fondly remembered professor of English: "The thing that cannot bear laughter is not a good thing." Mr. Thurber feels we should try more laughter on more things.

Readers of this newspaper may like to know that Mr. Thurber attributed to the *Christian Science Monitor* "one of the reasons I became a humorist." The story has been told before of how Mr. Thurber was paid for early contributions to the *Monitor* with checks made out to Jane Thurber. (In *The Year with Ross,* he recalls that his experience as "central Ohio correspondent" of the *Monitor* was one of the things that stuck in the mind of the late founder and editor of the *New Yorker,* Harold Ross, who said: "Thurber's worked too long on newspapers . . . He'll always write journalese.")

Eventually he wrote a letter of correction to the *Monitor.* The polite reply began: "Dear Miss Thurber . . . " This was back in the early twenties, when Mr. Thurber was covering, among other assignments, "new discoveries of the Mound Builders."

He went to interview a governor, who promptly said: "I never give out interviews to any sex."

"'Jane Thurber again,' I thought," Mr. Thurber recollected. But "sex" proved to be the governor's pronounciation of "sects." (Was this one of the confusions that inspired *The Case Book of James Thurber,* with its Gloucester man calling up the telephone sympathizer to make a complaint and its city editor sending reporter Thurber to watch a convention of oral surgeons operating on a mouse, which turned out to be a mouth?)

At any rate Mr. Thurber smiled as he described his term of being both male and female, enough perhaps to make anyone contemplate the humorous side of life.

Now when Mr. Thurber gets stuck or bored with a writing project, he leaves it temporarily and moves to another. In a recent rummaging through his files, Mrs. Thurber found some 37 unfinished pieces.

Among them she said, was one marked "Preface to Something. Hold."

"I'm thinking of using that for the title of my collected works," Mr. Thurber said.

The Secret Distractions of James Thurber
James Beizer/1959

From *The Hartford Courant Magazine,* August 30, 1959, p. 3.
Reprinted with permission of *The Hartford Courant.*

James Thurber, who has lived in Connecticut for 28 years, thinks that most of the people who live here don't know anything about the state.

He attributes this sad state of affairs to the fact that so many of them, especially the artists, writers, actors, and the like, are "pasted" on Connecticut and mostly come from other parts of the country.

"There are so many artists living in Connecticut now that you can't go up to a farmhouse for something like a glass of milk without getting an etching instead," he said.

"Most of them would be hard put to name the governor or Congressmen and other incidental facts. The only reason most of them live here is because it is close to New York City and doesn't have a state income tax. I guess it is the easiest place to live and work if you don't actually live in New York.

"This lack of knowledge of where you live isn't unusual," he went on. "When I went to England some years ago, I rented a car and drove around to look at all sorts of historic places. When I'd ask my English friends about them, they confess that they had never seen them, but could tell me all about Yellowstone and places like that in America where they had been but that I had never seen."

Thurber and his wife Helen live in a 14-room-house situated between the Mohawk State Forest and the famous Cathedral Pines in West Cornwall. Previously, Thurber had lived in many other Connecticut towns, such as Salisbury, Newtown, Sharon, Colebrook, Silvermine and Westport. In 1945, he bought his present home so that, among other reasons, his wife could be near her mother who lived in Bristol. Helen's father, the Rev. Ernest L. Wismer, was pastor for many years of the Congregational Church in that town.

The relative remoteness of West Cornwall was another factor which

68

prompted Thurber to buy a house there. For many years he also had an apartment in the Algonquin Hotel in New York but he found it was too difficult to get any work done there since "the telephone was always ringing and people were always dropping in."

The remoteness of a small Connecticut town, however, hasn't prevented one major intrusion on Thurber's peaceful existence: The mail still comes through. He estimates that he receives about 2,000 letters a year that demand answers. For this and his other more profitable writing, he is ably assisted by his wife and by his secretary, Mrs. Fritzi Von Keugeigen.

Since Thurber has been blind for some time, all this mail must be read to him. In addition, for example, he is also asked to do book reviews which is an equally slow reading process. When this article was written, he was at work on a review about the forthcoming biography of Groucho Marx.

There was also another minor distraction. His 27-year-old daughter and her husband Frederick Sauers and their two children, Sara 4, and Gregory 2, were visiting them.

"One of the previous owners of this house," Thurber commented, "died in an auto accident and another died during the war when the ship he was on sank. I suspect that my end will be brought about when I slip on a skate left on the stairs by my grandson, which just shows you how things have deteriorated since a writer moved in here."

Since his daughter and her family live in Western Springs, Ill., where her husband is employed by General Motors, this was the first time Thurber had met his grandson and according to Helen, was enjoying the visit tremendously.

Referring to Gregory, Thurber commented that the lad was "plenty of two-year-old." Quoting from George Bernard Shaw, he complained that it was a shame, youth and its vitality was wasted on the young.

He also mentioned that his daughter was expecting another child in the fall.

"All the young couples now seem to be having a lot more children than when I was their age. In the twenties, it seemed that people were too busy and of course, in the thirties when too many people had the time, they didn't have the money."

Still another intrusion into the quiet of Thurber's Connecticut life in recent months, since his latest book, *The Years with Ross,* was published, has been interviews and especially photographs.

"Nowadays they can't interview you without taking a couple of thousand pictures and after they are all through they call up and say they need some more. *Life* Magazine was around recently photographing everything in sight and occasionally me and they told me that only about 5 per cent of the pictures they take are ever used. Somewhere in New York there must be a gigantic warehouse containing nothing but pictures that never got into *Life*.

"Actually, I don't know why you want to interview me. Writers are the dullest people in the world. Ross (the late editor of the *New Yorker*) wouldn't allow a story in the magazine about a writer.

"I did hundreds of interviews for newspapers and the *New Yorker*, but they were of really interesting people—not writers. We ought to find you a murderer from the state prison which would make a much more interesting interview than me.

"Unfortunately, Americans are doing a tremendous amount of talking these days. Television is loaded with interview shows where people talk and talk about such uninteresting things that if you had to listen to them at the next table in a restaurant you would ask the waiter to find you a table on the other side of the room.

"What we seem to be developing is an oral culture of endless and uninteresting conversation. Why people want to listen to it is beyond me. And if it isn't the talk shows, it's the Western or detective bang-bangs.

"We've got three television sets around here and I sometimes listen to them, and after a couple of minutes, I could write the whole thing without half trying."

Considering Thurber's remarkable output over the years and his vast experience as a writer, this is hardly a hollow boast.

James Thurber was born in Columbus, Ohio, on Dec. 8, 1894. Following his graduation from Ohio State University, he worked as a code clerk at the American embassy in Paris from 1918-20. He returned to America in the latter year, began his writing career as a reporter on the *Columbus Dispatch*, where he was on the staff from 1920 to 1924 as a reporter for the European edition of the *Chicago Tribune*.

Two years later in 1926, he invaded New York and was hired as a reporter for the *New York Evening Post*. In 1927, he began his long association with the *New Yorker,* which was started two years before by his late friend Harold Ross.

For seven years, until 1935, Thurber was on the regular staff of the magazine. He wrote "The Talk of The Town," and performed many other editorial chores, such as covering tennis.

Thurber was married to Helen, who is his second wife, in 1935 and in the same year left the regular staff of the *New Yorker* to freelance, although most of his stories continued to be written for the *New Yorker.*

Helen was the editor of several "pulp" magazines before her marriage and, according to Thurber, she is a tremendous help to him in his writing.

"She does a lot of my editing and proof-reading, and is very good at it," he said. "She caught many things in my latest book, which would have been ridiculous if they had remained the way the publisher had them. Publishers edit books so badly, that unless a writer has a good editor in his house, he's up against a great handicap."

Including *The Years with Ross*, which has been number two on the best-seller list for many weeks, Thurber has written 23 books and thousands of articles. Some have been turned into plays and movies and recently many have been adapted for television. He is also famous as an artist, and his pictures of dogs are classics. Since he lost his eyesight, he no longer does any drawing.

He might not care for the title but Thurber today is probably the dean of American humor writers.

Always a Newspaper Man

Robert Vincent/1959

From *The Columbus Dispatch Magazine,* December 14, 1959, pp. 46-47. Reprinted with permission of *The Columbus Dispatch.*

To the entire English-speaking world, which delights in his pixie-like humor and his outrageous line drawings of men, women and dogs— which all seem to have a loosely filled potato sack for a universal model—he is the foremost humorist of our time.

To sophisticated New York, he is James Thurber, artist, playwright, author of 23 successful books, bon vivant, speaker, friend of the mighty, hail-fellow-well-met.

To newspapermen in Columbus, however, he insists on being plain Jim Thurber, one-time City Hall reporter for the *Dispatch* and—he admits with delightful candor—still "a helluva good newspaperman."

For to this cosmopolitan, Columbus is still home, Ohio State University still his Alma Mater. The *Dispatch* still the newspaper to which he ungrudgingly gives a part of his heart.

With his amazing "total recall" memory—which he now uses as an adequate substitute for the eyes which failed him completely in 1951, when he drew his last cartoon—he remembers vividly the day in January, 1921, when fire destroyed the old City Hall, where the Ohio Theater now stands.

"Bob Kanode of the *Citizen* and I were sitting out a council meeting in the press room when a battalion chief stuck his head in the door and hollered, 'Hey, you guys get out of here. The building's on fire!'

"We got out an extra on that one—and I got a $5 raise."

Thurber the reporter, who was born at 251 Parsons Avenue, stayed with the *Dispatch* for four years before he moved to greener, lusher pastures—newspapers in Paris, Nice and New York before going with the *New Yorker* magazine.

He joined the *Dispatch* before he finished his classes at OSU— where his classmate was Elliott Nugent, with whom he collaborated on the immortal *Male Animal*—and at first didn't get along at all well with the then city editor, Norman "Gus" Kuchner, later to become his good and close friend.

"I was hired by the managing editor while Gus was on vacation," Thurber recalls with a chuckle. "He called me 'Phi Beta Kappa' because I went to college. We didn't really get along good until I told him I didn't graduate."

Thurber's inimitable style later won him honorary degrees from Kenyon, Williams and Yale, but it is still Ohio State that he calls his college.

His early days as a newsman weren't easy ones.

"Whenever I'm in the Midwest, I still wake up with a start, wondering what time it is and thinking I have to cover City Hall by one o'clock," he reminisces.

"After 36 years, my anxiety dreams are still about the *Dispatch*, where I'm with no paper, no pencils, a typewriter that won't work, Gus glaring over my shoulder, and the clock frozen at ten minutes to one—with one o'clock the deadline."

Thurber looks at you directly and is such an ardent conversationalist that you soon forget that now he is totally blind. He has a nervous habit of running his left hand through his gray, leonine hair, lights his own cigarettes which he chain-smokes, and manages to place his guests, be they prince or peasant, completely at ease within minutes of meeting them.

His fantastic memory enables him to recall, for instance, the membership of the entire city council which met that fateful night, as well as the names of all city officials and even every single member of the *Dispatch* staff.

He uses that memory to "write" in his brain entire articles which he then "recites" to his secretary in stretches of 500 to 1000 words at a time. He can recall word for word, his latest articles in the *New Yorker.*

When he is in New York, he dictates—or "recites"—to a secretary for about three hours at a time. But on the road his only traveling companion is his wife, Helen.

She is his eyes.

This long, thin man, whose works bid fair to become immortal and whose humor was described by Stephen Vincent Benét "as

unmistakable as a kangaroo," is proud above all other accomplish-
ments of being a newspaperman.

"I got 17 steamer headlines when I was on the *Dispatch*," he says.
And there is more than a touch of wistfulness and nostalgia in his
voice.

"You call me Jim if you're a newspaperman. You show me a
newspaperman who wants another newspaperman to call him
'mister,' and I'll show you a newspaperman who wasn't worth a
damn in the first place."

James Thurber Modifies Views (A Bit)

Judd Arnett/1960

From *The Detroit Free Press,* January 12, 1960. Reprinted with permission of *The Detroit Free Press.*

One of the greatest nonconformists of the modern era may be mellowing a bit.

James Thurber, author, artist, playwright and rebel came to Detroit Monday and said a few kind words about women.

He didn't go overboard in favor of them, understand.

Still, he recanted to the point of admitting that "women are good critics."

This, as Thurber fans will no doubt agree, is almost heresy from the man who has spent a fruitful lifetime developing one central theme: "The domination of the American male by the American female."

What was it he wrote in 1950? "I consider the American Woman the greatest potential power in the world and altogether too complacent and lazy to do anything about it."

He has weakened a bit, hasn't he?

But in all other fronts, he remains the James Thurber of old, high in his hopes for the theater of today and tomorrow, and full of delightful animosity for those who would fit all America to a common mold.

His play, *A Thurber Carnival,* opens Tuesday night at the Shubert Theater as part of its pre-Broadway run and by his own admission "there is still a good deal of work to be done on it."

However, this work won't be hindered by Thurber's love for his own prose.

"The printed page is not the speaking stage," he said. "No play in history has ever been put on without change in the original script, and this one certainly won't be."

By his own description, Thurber is "now blind and 65," and he admits to being handicapped by his inability to see the visual effects of his work.

But he retains "the best of all indicators"—the ability to hear audience reaction.

"I still believe that the audience knows best," he said. "If you don't pay attention to the reaction of the people who have paid to see and hear your play, you're crazy."

One of the few authors who refused to take the "McCarthyism" of the early 1950s seriously, Thurber is still bitterly opposed to what he considers the attempt to make all Americans "conform."

"This country was founded by controversial people," he insisted, "and conformity is not a part of our true heritage.

"Too many Americans," he continued, "are motivated by fear. If we have no faith but what we are afraid of, then we are sunk."

Part of the "unconscious effect" of fear, he said, shows up in modern comedy "which has become louder and more jumpy."

Then, just to show that he doesn't "fear" women, either, he concluded: "All the women I have ever known, dislike history. They think it is not only dull, but dreadful."

The "old Thurber" speaking, thank goodness.

Pupils Delighted by Thurber—
They Laughed, They Listened

The Cincinnati Post & Times-Star/1960

From *The Cincinnati Post & Times-Star,* February 12, 1960, p. 41.
Reprinted with permission of *The Cincinnati Post.*

He made you laugh and think. Then slowly his spirit got into your veins.

You watched him fumble for the matches on the desk, wipe his brow, ramble on from subject to subject, idea to idea.

He quoted people you never heard of, tossed in thoughts you didn't quite grasp and spoke in a soft voice you had to strain to hear. But it was explosively soft.

He was humorist James Thurber, 65, blind, sitting in a lounging chair, wearing an open blue sports shirt. Around him on the floor were 40 bright-eyed high school English students. He couldn't see them.

But, Mr. Thurber, they were listening.

"There are two conventions in this hotel and on the elevators the men tell jokes," he said. "HA-HA-HA-HA, GUFFAW-GUFFAW! Everybody bellylaughs. It deafens you."

"A woman reads her newspaper and says, 'Why can't Walter Lippman be more cheerful? Doesn't he know it will all work out in the end?' We Americans must have invented that idea."

"In the wonderful cartoon strip, 'Penny,' the girl says, 'Gee, wish I had better taste than to watch television.' It's up to her to get it."

His mind leaps to education.

"I read Henry James and Edith Wharton before I was 12 years old," Thurber said. "Now families take the books away because their children are too young. That's silly.

"Boys in England and France know more at 15 than ours do at 22.

"Margaret Mead talks about the house husband. He gets engaged or married in college, with no money or nothing in mind, and goes from college to kitchen. He doesn't have experience.

77

"A girl gets married at 18, has three children by 26 and at 32 finds she doesn't know anything. 'What am I going to do?' she asks. She can't do anything so—she has more children."

Several things bother James Thurber.

Fear.

Sentimentality.

Loudness.

Complacency.

"And inaccuracy," he says. "As I tour from city to city, I'm shocked at the decay of American journalism. There's no concern for precision. And there's no initiative. 'Don't get it right; get it written.' "

He wishes "good luck" to those who try to analyze humor.

"Psychologists try to study the creative process," he says. Freud stopped when he came to talent and humor. E. B. White says, 'Humor is like anything else. It can be dissected but something dies in the process.'

"If you're a writer, you write. If you're not, you can't."

The McCarthy era has no spot in Thurber's heart.

"While the Communists were sweeping the world, we were becoming suspicious of ourselves, investigating every nook and cranny of our schools, churches, theaters," he says.

"By refusing the Communists the right to speak, we created the idea that maybe they have something to say.

"If we let them speak, we'd find out they're wrong.

"In England," Thurber continues, "you can meet the members of all parties. The English say, 'Here's our Communist friend. He's terribly wrong. But he's a nice chap.'

"Americans seem to think they have a monopoly on patriotism. Actually we don't have a clear idea of what it means. You don't hear of any un-French Frenchmen, un-German Germans or un-Italian Italians. America is still a young country."

Thurber had other comments to make about America:

• "Mr. Nixon had an article recently in the *Saturday Review of Literature* in which he said we must develop an anti-Communist faith. Doesn't he realize we can't have a negative faith? Faith must be affirmative. You can't introduce negation into love. We must believe in something."

• "It's the American idea that the louder you laugh, the funnier something is. I think it's the other way around."

• "Will Rogers is remembered as America's greatest 'Oh, Shucks' philosopher. The truth is Rogers used political satire as vaudeville. Somebody told him, 'Why not make fun of Congress?' So he did. He spoke from the top of his head and not the bottom of his heart."

Thurber says he gets letters from high school students all the time.

"They say, 'Dear Mr. Thurber . . . I have chosen you as my favorite American writer. I am doing a paper on you and I would like your answer to a few questions: What did you write? What is your kind of humor?'

"I answer the one letter in 50 that is intelligent."

Mrs. Thurber asked a few of the still-hungry high school students to leave so James could do some writing. Mr. Thurber's voice trailed off as everyone left.

His memory lingered on.

Thurber Intends to Relax till '61

Arthur Gelb/1960

From *The New York Times*, Monday, March 28, 1960, p. 35.
Copyright © 1960 by The New York Times Company. Reprinted
by permission.

James Thurber, whose *Carnival* is one of Broadway's biggest hits, is a
man who intends doing his utmost to reach the age of at least 80 with
his faculties more or less intact. One of the ways in which he plans to
attain longevity is by avoiding too frequent contact with show business. He will stay out of the theatre, he said, until "at least the fall of
1961."

Naturally, as the author of a Broadway success, he is being
importuned to follow it up quickly with another entry, and he has on
hand two items that could be whipped into shape immediately, if he
chose to whip them, and himself. But he does not choose.

"I have a play and another revue," he admitted yesterday at his
home in West Cornwall, Conn. The play, called *Make My Bed,* is
about Harold Ross and the *New Yorker,* and the revue will contain
original sketches Mr. Thurber wrote for *A Thurber Carnival* but
finished too late to insert in the show.

"I'm not going to get either of them ready for a while," he said. "I
can't understand how anyone can do two shows in succession for
Broadway, without doing something more restful in between—I
mean something for the printed page."

Mr. Thurber has been ill and convalescing since the day following
the Feb. 26 opening of *A Thurber Carnival.*

"I came down with a throat infection, accompanied by natural
exhaustion following a seven-week tryout in six cities," he said. "The
theatre goes too fast for me. I'm 65 and I'm not a 600-mile-an-hour,
jet-propelled writer.

"That's the trouble with this country. A man has a success on
Broadway—or anywhere else, for that matter—and he feels he has to
follow it up quickly with another success. It's the American disease of
jet propulsion. Look how they're dying off!

"Thirty-two men on the New Yorker have died since I went to work there in 1927. Two-thirds of the old Algonquin group is gone. Stanley Walker and I recently counted 130 men we knew in the writing field who had died under the age of 64. This is probably the only country in the world that has only two writers—Carl Sandburg and Robert Frost—still working in their eighties."

Aside from the wear and tear of a Broadway production, said Mr. Thurber, he really derives more pleasure from "polishing my own sentences in my own room, than collaborating with fifteen people in a theatre."

"I always have been a careful writer," he added. "I am a perfectionist. I've often spent as much as a year and a half writing something, and then thrown it away. When I get stuck in writing, I draw. I like to take my time."

Indicating that such an attitude is given short shrift in the theatre, Mr. Thurber recalled that during the tryout of The Male Animal in 1940, the producer, Herman Shamin, said to him:

"You're obviously dissatisfied. What do you want to do?"

"Spend another year working on the play," said Mr. Thurber.

"Dammit, we open next Monday in New York," replied Mr. Shumlin, ending the conversation.

Mr. Thurber's present project for the printed page is a 30,000-word satire called "The Nightinghoul," which concerns the returned descent upon a city of a large, mechanized flying creature.

"What I am trying to say," Mr. Thurber explained, "is that people will find it necessary to create a creature, or an evil, where one doesn't exist, so that they can get the credit for creating it. This is a time when we want to believe, not know, we want to take things for granted, not find out about them.

"I don't think anyone should write comedy nowadays that is pure nonsense; it must have meaning. I'm always astounded when my humor is described as gentle. It's anything but that, and I intend to beat up the next person who says that about me."

Thurber Gives Advice to American Women

Virginia Haufe/1960

From *Ohioana*, Summer, 1960, pp. 34-36. Reprinted with permission of the Martha Kinney Cooper Ohioana Library Association.

"You were born in March," announced Mr. Thurber as I entered his suite at the Hotel Carter.

"Yes, that's right," I said in amazement. "But how did you know?"

"Oh, guessing the month people were born in is a hobby of mine."

I settled myself in the chair next to his and began scribbling furiously in my stenographer's notebook. Mr. Thurber's thoughts came so rapidly that it was difficult for me to keep up with him.

"Young people come to me and say they want to be a writer," he began. "They ask me why do you write? If you can ask that question, you're not a writer and never will be. You might just as well ask that of a surgeon or a scientist.

"I am constantly appalled by the letters students write to me. Usually they go like this: Our class has been asked to select an American writer as a subject. I like everything you have ever written. Please answer the following questions—what have you written?

"They usually finish by asking me to send them a signed photograph of myself. Teachers are making autograph hounds and photograph collectors out of kids.

"A student from a high school in New York wrote, 'Please tell me how to dedicate a book.' Can't he look inside one and find out? If they can't even dedicate a book, how are they going to write one? They're dedicating something they'll never write."

At this point I thought I had better ask him a few of the questions on my list.

"Mr. Thurber, I heard you wrote the original version of 'The Day the Dam Broke' for the *Sun Dial*. Could you tell me something about that?"

"No, no, that's not correct. I graduated from Ohio State in 1919. I didn't write 'The Day the Dam Broke' until 1933. It first appeared in the *New Yorker* and is included in *My Life and Hard Times,* which is my most famous book."

Mr. Thurber then launched into one of his favorite topics—the American girl.

"I don't think the American girl much cares about knowledge. She is interested only in her home town and her home state. She should show a wider interest than that.

"The average woman knows nothing about history, economics, or foreign trade. A short time ago, I dictated this sentence to my secretary in New York. 'I don't know any woman that likes history.' By a Freudian slip, she put down, 'I don't like any woman that likes history.'

"All girls want is money, clothes, boyfriends.

"In my day all girls quit school as sophomores to get married. Now they quit earlier. Those that do stay are in the dramatic clubs or on the magazines . . . something that's fun.

"Most girls marry at 18; they have three children at twenty-six. When they're about 32 they become frantic because they realize they don't know much. Then they start taking adult education courses. By that time it may be too late.

"These days girls and boys give up their youth and their activities to plunge into being housewives and househusbands. Where would we have been if Lewis and Clark or Daniel Boone had done the same? How would we have found the Northwest passage or got through to California?

"All the intellectual women in the country are worried to death about the househusband. A househusband is a man who gets home from work and bathes and feeds the babies.

"This means declining masculinity in the sense of opportunities for natural adventure, and being outdoors, tramping in the woods. He should be putting engines together and taking them apart. Instead he's bathing babies and wearing an apron."

"Mr. Thurber," I interjected, "I saw a program on television a few months ago about Moscow University. Over half the students are women and they're studying math and physics. Do you think this will make the Russian woman less feminine?"

"No, not at all. All you have to do is look at their great troupe of dancers. I met a Russian ballerina not too long ago. She said if she had it to do all over again she'd become an engineer.

"Don't think that because a woman gets off the couch she's going to lose her femininity.

"Too much attention is given to attracting the males and making other women envious. I don't think that wearing too much make-up and stiletto heels makes a woman feminine. It just makes her look foolish.

"Women should go ahead. They live longer and are stronger physically. The average man in the arts and literature dies at 50. The women go on forever. It's shocking how young the American man dies."

Mr. Thurber feels a woman should be a real helpmate to her husband.

"My wife is a graduate of Mt. Holyoke. She married me at 32; it was her first marriage. She was an editor for ten years. Greatest proofreader and editor I know of. Her mother is from Scotland and her father is from Canada. Maybe that's the reason for it.

"She's a woman that helps her husband. Also runs the house. She handles all the accounts, the bank, income, proofs of manuscripts, servants, everything."

He paused for a few moments, then continued:

"Can you define the word freedom?"

I hesitated, trying to put my thoughts into words.

"You ought to learn," he went on. "Freedom is not just the right to do what you want to, from buying your own kind of chewing gum to choosing your own hairdresser. It has to be fought for every day.

"Those of us who spend any time abroad are appalled by our lack of direction, our complacency, our belief that everything is going to be all right.

"Russian society is a purposeful society. Ours is not. The Russians remind me of a crowd at a football game all cheering together. Americans remind me of people scattered at a picnic, each having his own fun. But people don't think about it or worry about it."

"Well, what should we do?" I queried.

"Don't come to my generation for a solution. Yours is the generation that has to think of a solution.

"You saw A Thurber Carnival last night?"

"Yes, and I loved it. Especially 'If Grant Had Been Drinking at Appomattox.' "

"About the Grant skit. A woman said to me, 'I don't like the bastardization of history.' That woman didn't know the point of the thing and she didn't know history.

"And I don't like my humor to be called mild and gentle. I'm laying in wait for the next person that calls me elfin. If it's a man, I'll propose to kick him to death."

The conversation turned to a discussion of humor in general.

"Americans think they're a humorous nation and they're not. We're nowhere near as basically humorous as the English. A belly laugh is our idea of humor. Americans don't want things that cause them to chuckle or smile—they want to slap each other on the back. Yet they think that Americans have the greatest sense of humor in the world.

"Americans don't like to be criticized. This is unfortunate. If you can't make fun of yourself and laugh at your own institutions and people you're lost."

Ere I departed, I asked Mr. Thurber if I might take his photo. He gave his permission, but first warned me,

"Be careful of photography. It gets to be like dope. First you take just two pictures, then you want to take the whole roll. A photographer in France spent the whole day taking my picture. Mad as a hatter. Most photographers are."

After taking two pictures of Mr. Thurber, I took my leave. He's a fascinating conversationalist and a charming and gracious person.

Antic Disposition

W. J. Weatherby/1961

From *The Manchester Guardian*, February 2, 1961, p. 9. Reprinted with permission of *The Manchester Guardian* and the author.

There were no dogs, not even floppy bloodhounds, in the London hotel room. James Thurber sat alone, his four senses so active that our five felt disgraced. His eyes did not look blind behind his glasses, they had not got that look of eyes washed in milk that many blind people's have, and he found his whiskey and his cigarettes unerringly: a real "pro" at overcoming the handicaps of blindness as at everything else.

Some of Thurber's fans might have expected to find a Seeing Eye dog reposing at his feet, those fans—or nonreaders as Thurber might call them—who think of dogs and Thurber as inseparable. Thurber himself feels as though he is dogged by his dogs. People who meet him gush about how much they love his "charming dogs" and his "lovely cartoons," while the gloomy social critic, the superb prose writer, fumes behind his glasses, behind the little moustache that seems to bristle with indignation.

He looks like one of his own characters, *My Life and Hard Times* 20 years later: a tall, lean man thinned down by the worry of the war between men and women, his moustache an overcivilised patch that any caveman would scorn. But he does not talk like a Thurber man: his talk is a constant stream that in 66 years must have added up to a whole sea, for Thurber is one of the greatest talkers in America. It seems incredible that he has had the time to write such a large and varied body of work as well—and he writes slowly, a rebuke to the satisfied-first-time school. He calls himself not a writer but a "rewriter": the finished book lies somewhere between the fifth and fifteenth versions, the prose style by then giving an impression of effortlessness but without any hint of glibness . . .

Blind and unable to see his words, he composes in his head—that memory again—and continually fears that sloppiness may creep back while he is not looking. A reporter who created a modern prose style—this evolution seems one of his greatest achievements. His view of the world is thus admirably expressed, that view of a twentieth-century man gripped in a panic that drives him into all kinds of odd antics. The quick reader sees the antics and thinks Thurber a funny man—"a clown," as he says bitterly. Underneath, of course, there is often as much pessimism as in Faulkner. And in conversation what he says is often deeply gloomy, and yet—like his work—is expressed with such verve and pell-mell vitality that the final impression is optimistic, of a man engaged in life to the hilt, whose desperation comes from seeing so many missed opportunities for living.

He certainly has not missed many himself. Blind in his left eye since boyhood, totally blind for the last ten years, he has added acting to a long list of activities and has come over to London to write a book or two, a play or two, and to repeat his Broadway performance in *The Thurber Carnival*. And of course to talk. That day in the London hotel he needed hardly any questions, pouring out what seemed like part of the interior monologue that has been going on now for 66 years:

"All Americans are going 600 miles an hour jet-propelled. But where to? I know one man who is so afraid of being alone that he takes a portable radio to the bathroom. They ask me what I do in a room just sitting there and when I say, 'Meditate,' they think I need a psychiatrist . . . . "

Interviewer: "I heard you sometimes write at parties—."

Thurber: "That's right. Helen will come up and say, 'Thurber, stop writing. That girl has been talking to you for ten minutes and you never even realised she was there.' I have to admit I was preoccupied because I had just realised how to get out of a certain paragraph. People seem to think I'm just a funny man, a dog man. I haven't done any drawings since I went blind but they still ask me how my dogs are coming along. Some people even think I make jokes about dogs. For God's sake anybody who looks at my drawings with enough observation should be able to see the dogs play the part of intelligence and repose. Typical of the stupidity of our own species was my woman who said, 'If I rang the wrong number, why did you answer the phone?' That seems typical of the female intelligence,

though I do get some intelligent letters from women. Notice the
despair and resignation of the dog in that picture. Oh, I've been
writing about the ego for 30 years and I'm still taken for a
clown . . . .

"You know—there's another 'you know'—I'm going to be busy
over here. The greatest hyphen link—that's what I call the Anglo-
American world. The British and the Americans have always argued
like a family, but the most important thing in our world is for us to
stick together . . . "

When he mentioned a name he would carefully spell it; his
monologue itself sometimes seemed like an act of courtesy to save a
fellow newspaperman from having to ask any questions. One tried a
question or two, but they were like logs swept away down a flooding
river, the answers appearing minutes and many paragraphs later.
When at last the Thurber monologue paused, one said goodbye with
thanks for the chance to tune in on it. He beamed and when last
seen was sitting back on the couch. Had he started writing again?

Blind at 67, Thurber Still Cracks the Wit

Eddy Gilmore/1961

From *The Toledo Blade,* May 7, 1961, pp. 1, 2. Reprinted with permission of The Associated Press.

LONDON (AP)—"I didn't say the American male is a panther," explained James Thurber, "I said he's a pouncer. There's a lot of difference between a panther and a pouncer. The American approach is to pounce."

The 67-year-old author, now totally blind but busier than ever, speaks in a sort of trans-American accent—basically Middle West with faint overlays from the more effete eastern seaboard.

But there's nothing effete about Jim Thurber.

"I was once in a taxi with a girl," he went on, "and she said to me, 'You're the first American who hasn't pounced on me,' and I said to her, 'I have my gentle approach—and I've also got my front teeth.' "

Talking with Mr. Thurber is always a memorable experience. It's hard to report him in conventional forms, though. His wonderful rush of words raises hell with punctuation.

The great man doesn't talk in staid block paragraphs. Instead, he sweeps along in a superb flow of adult and witty observation, well laced with un-angry iron.

Like this:

"The great thing about women today is that they're beginning to take a little interest in sex whereas the men are beginning to take little interest in anything else . . . the perfect woman? Huh . . . There's no such thing, thank God . . . But the qualities I most admire in women are beauty, ardor, humor and, of course—wealth . . . I wish I could remember the name of the bright person who once said 'A woman's place is in the wrong.' . . . Wouldn't it be marvelous to see Mrs. Khrushchev take over from Mr. Khrushchev? After his performance at the United Nations, I said to somebody, 'great oafs from little ikons grow.' . . . Yes, sir . . . A man always marries the woman of her choice."

89

He ran his long thin fingers through his thick mop of iron-gray and
somehow—instinctively—seemed aware that the waiter was standing
behind him. He cut the air with the hand he didn't have in his hair
and politely asked the man to bring another round of drinks.

Mr. Thurber's talk is far from a monologue, but playing straight
man to him is one of the easiest and most pleasant jobs.

"Me a writer? . . . Huh . . . I used to be a reporter. Back in
Columbus, Ohio . . . You couldn't call me a writer now. I'm more of
a re-writer.

" . . . The finished book—my finished book. It lies somewhere
between the 5th and 15th version . . . "

His voice faded off for a moment as he leaned forward and again
seemed instinctively to know where the small unbeautiful hotel lobby
ash tray stood.

"You ask me about total recall . . . Yep, I've got it all right . . . I can
remember a dream I had in 1910, and I once told a girl she was
wrong about a dress she wore 22 years before . . . "

The head waiter tip-toed up and motioned with his eyebrows that
the dinner was ready in the dining room about 25 yards away.

Mr. Thurber rose and with an almost imperceptible gesture
touched the sleeve of my left arm. I moved towad the dining room
and with the grace of one of Ohio State's more deft-footed halfbacks
following his interference, the blind man quickly followed me into the
dining room.

This man who looks 15 years younger than his age discusses
blindness with a light and airy objectivity.

"Well, it has its compensations, you know. If I could see, I might go
into a room and say to myself, 'My god, there's that dreadful Mrs.
Norman across the room. How'm I going to avoid her?' But you see,
I don't see her . .

The wine waiter set before him a fourth-filled glass of white.

Mr. Thurber reached forward and knew exactly where the glass
stood.

"And I remember where I put it down," he said in what could only
have been something awfully close to mind-reading.

"Mental telepathy? Of course I believe in it. I've proved it time and
again. A woman once asked me about it and I said to her—and I said

it all in one breath—take a number from 1 to 20—and don't look surprised when I tell you it's five. It was five, too . . . "

Somebody asked him, "What's wrong with America?"

After downing an oyster, he replied, "I don't know, but it's something. It's like I say about Loch Ness—there is something out there . . . Well, something's wrong over there, but I'll be back. Of course I will . . . You see I'm over here to do the *Thurber Carnival.* Acted in it in New York, you remember. Well, I don't know when they're going to put it on over here . . .

"Helen (Mrs. Thurber) said to me 'I packed for six months before we came over here and I'm damned if I'm going to start packing all over again' . . . In America, the men are going 600 miles an hour all the time jet-propelled. But where to? I know a man who's so afraid of being alone that he takes a portable radio with him into the bathroom . . . People ask me what I do in a room alone and when I say 'I meditate,' they think I need a psychiatrist . . . "

This tends to give the impression that he does all the talking, which is wrong. He listens and asks questions, but he's such a marvelous talker that he somehow makes it all weave together.

An actress at the table made an acid remark about a certain producer and asked Mr. Thurber what he thought of the man.

"I can understand most writers," he replied, "a few publishers—but no producers."

The pretty actress shrieked with delight.

"Women are the greatest power on earth," he said taking oral wings again, "but the sad thing is their lack of cooperation . . . One woman meets another. They both run their eyes over the other's clothes, but they don't see what's really there. What's in the other's brain. Why, if they're the greatest power on earth, don't they get together?"

Mr. Thurber arrived in London on his present visit Jan. 25. He's presently trying to write a new play and two new books, but the difficulty is finding the time.

The British press—and the American newsmen stationed in London too—take up a great deal of his time and, being an old newspaperman, he can't bring himself to saying "no" when they want to interview him.

Recently, when he was getting an average of 25 requests a day from newspapers, magazines and television and radio, he moved in quiet desperation to the country.

Now, he's back in London half-incognito. That is, he lets only about half of the calls reach him.

The Tulle and Taffeta Rut:
A Conversation with James Thurber

Henry Brandon/1961

Originally published under the title "Everybody Is Getting Se-rious" in *New Republic,* May 26, 1958. Reprinted and expanded in Brandon's *As We Are* (Garden City, N.Y.: Doubleday, 1961). This version is from *As We Are,* pp. 257-282. Copyright © 1960, 1961 by Henry Brandon. Reprinted by permission of Doubleday, a division of Bantam, Doubleday, Dell Publishing Group, Inc.

Remembering the melancholy end of James Thurber's story "The Interview," I approached an interview with him not without trepidation. Would mine too end with pencil and notebook thrown out of the window? Or, worse still in my particular case, would the tape recorder be flung out into the street?

What made me even more nervous in my eager expec-tation was the fear of an anticlimax. Everybody thought that Thurber was a "natural" for my type of conversation piece. Yet at the back of my mind I remembered how often I had found professional humorists to be disappointingly unfunny in conversation. Finally, knowing from his writing how much he hates gadgets, wondered how he would react to the presence of my tape recorder.

It was with these anxious thoughts that I knocked at the door of Thurber's suite at the venerable Hotel Algonquin in his habitual pied-a-terre whenever he comes to town from his retreat in Connecticut.

My anxieties, however, were quickly dispelled by Thurber himself and his dedicated wife Helen. They made me feel at ease in no time, even though Thurber's gaunt figure and his flat, commanding voice were a little intim-idating at first. This was not the "little-man-what-now" type trapped between the "hard covers" of life, this was a man who knew what he wanted, who had learned and obviously succeeded in overcoming many vicissitudes of life. He had read an earlier conversation piece of mine with Leonard Bernstein and obviously impressed by Bernstein's performance, wondered aloud whether he would be able to do as well. Now it became my turn to reassure him, to put him at ease. A human situation in the best Thurber style had evolved.

Helen quietly left after a while and Thurber without any prodding began to talk about himself, about his ideas. The interview did not begin with a question: it just happened. We were talking and I switched on the tape recorder . . . My earlier fears proved completely unfounded. Not only was Jim a relaxed conversationalist with a humor that slays with the touch of a feather, but he also seemed completely unconcerned about my tape recorder. At least that was my impression that afternoon.

However twelve hours later, and in all fairness to Jim, I must mention this; he sent a three-page, single-spaced letter to my room which began as follows:

> In the watches of the night I began remembering recent verbal assaults I have made, when in a bad mood, upon the craze for interviews. My opposition lies in the fact that offhand answers have little value or grace of expression, and that such oral give and take help to perpetuate the decline of the English language in my country and yours . . . While lying awake around dawn this morning I began polishing some of the things I told you. Since I rewrite everything all the way through from five to twenty times it is hard for me to think of my conversational replies being used as my final considered opinions and judgments. Maybe it will come out all right, but here are a few written thoughts . . .

I sat down immediately and listened to the tape, then compared it to his letter. There was no doubt in my mind that the tape was much better than the content of his letter. And in the end he agreed.

Thurber is one of the oldest members of *The New Yorker* staff, and his stories and fables have made him perhaps the most important writer of serious comedy today. His humor has a universal quality because it springs from the inadequacies, the pathos, the inevitabilities, and the tragedies of the human situation. Nothing is more difficult than to make you laugh at the truth. But that is Thurber's great gift. He also makes you think. There is always something serious, something moving hidden between the lines. It is a humor touched, often soaked, in melancholy. It is devastating in a quiet way and so are his drawings of the bewildered human race. Since his first book, which he wrote with E. B. White, *Is Sex Necessary?*, he had written some two dozen others, his latest being his reminiscences of Harold Ross, the fabulous character who founded *The New Yorker.*

The total blindness which has enveloped Thurber for some years now has made it impossible for him to continue drawing his whimsical cartoons. Today, the only thing he can still draw in a sort of mechanical way, is his dog. He showed me how. He placed the fingers of his left hand on a paper in an obviously well-rehearsed position and then he led his pencil carefully from one finger to another. The connecting lines between the fingers surprisingly added up to a perfect outline of a dog's head. But in order to place its eye in the right spot his wife had to come to his aid. He lives now in a diffusion of light. But the eyes of his mind are sharper than those of most seeing people. Thurber's real secret however is a warm heart and an angry mind.

Thurber: . . . One of my great English friends was the late Paul Nash, your great painter and critic. Paul came over here in 1931 as one of the three foreign judges of the Annual Carnegie Museum of Arts Painting Show, of all places in Pittsburgh, and I had lunch with him at the Century Club, not realizing that the forefront of American art would be there, all the great American painters. Nash had never heard of any of them. I'd only been drawing for about two years but he came to see me and said: "You're Thurber." And he insisted on having me put at his right, whereupon I got so nervous I grabbed a bottle of Scotch from the sideboard and put that on my left between us. Then he said to a distinguished bearded connoisseur of art across the table: "Do you know Milt Gross?" And the man said: "Never heard of him."

Of course, Paul was what I call in one of my pieces, Admirer-in-Chief of American comic art. In this piece I tell about one incident in London twenty years ago . . . I had a one-man show of drawings to my own amazement. Nash, of course, came around. One wonderful thing was that two of the drawings were stolen; the gallery boys were frantic about this but I was pleased mightily that anybody would risk arrest or, at least, reprimand for stealing some of my drawings. After all, if you have your drawings stolen, you're made.

Nevertheless *The New Yorker* turned down a series of mine called
"The Patient"—about ten drawings of a man in the hospital. Shortly
thereafter they were printed in a London magazine no longer in
existence called *Night and Day.* Do you remember *Night and Day?* I
sent the prints to Ross, the then editor of *The New Yorker.* He then
decided that definitely I was just a passing fad—"the fancy of the
English" as he said, but he became very proud that the English knew
about *The New Yorker.*

Nash had said in one piece in the *New Statesman* about comic art
that "Thurber seems to start drawing with nothing in mind—just
scrawling as in the early style of Henri Matisse." Word of mouth
changed this into the fact—the supposed fact—that Matisse admired
my drawings. He happened to be in London, the old gentleman, in
'37 or '38, when I was, so they called him up to see if they could
arrange a meeting. But the gallery man who called up his secretary
came back pale and stammering and said: "Mr. Matisse's secretary
says that he had never heard of Mr. Thurber OR *The New Yorker.*"
That delighted me to no end and I innocently sent a telegram off to
Ross that Matisse had never heard of Thurber OR *The New Yorker.*
Ross had never heard of Matisse, so that evened things up.

Brandon: What does really inspire you to sit down and draw?

Thurber: Well, actually, it was a thing just like lighting this
cigarette, I think . . . it was a form of relaxation after writing, or when
I got stuck on a piece of writing. A great many of the drawings I did, I
was unconscious of doing. It was only in 1929 when I shared an office with E. B. White at *The New Yorker* that he began to pick up my
drawings—pencil drawings on yellow copy paper—and then, I think
in April 1929, sent one to *The New Yorker* art meeting. I'd done it in
about thirteen seconds—a seal on a rock gazing at two distant specks
and saying: "Hmm—explorers."

Well, Ross thought it was a gag—Rea Irvin, our art editor, drew on
my drawing, up in the corner, a head of a seal—Rea being a professional artist and great draftsman—and wrote under it, still on my
drawing: "This is the way a seal's whiskers go." Andy White promptly
the next Tuesday—we had an art meeting every Tuesday—sent it
back with a note saying: "This is the way a Thurber seal's whiskers
go." They still rejected it.

Then White and I wrote *Is Sex Necessary?*—a burlesque and

parody on the flocks of sex books coming out at the time. We took the drawings to the publisher and laid them out on the floor, and three members of the firm of Harper's stared at them and said: "These are, we presume, a rough idea of what you'd like a professional artist to do for the book." And White said: "No, these are the drawings that go in the book." Well, that really shook them—they almost brought the book out quietly.

But then, to everbody's amazement, including Ross's, it began to sell, and he heard about it—and about the drawings—and he came into my office and said: "Where's that damned seal drawing you did—several months ago—that White sent in." And I said: "Where is it? You rejected it, so I threw it away." And he said: "Don't throw things away just because I don't like them—or think I don't. Do it again!"

Well, I didn't do it again for two years. And when I did do it again, by sheer accident, it became the best known of all my drawings. In trying to draw the seal on a rock again with pen and ink—and the seal was just the same as ever with Thurber seal's whiskers—the rock looked more like the head of a bed. So I finished the bed, put a man and his wife in it and had the woman snarling at her husband: "All right, have it your way—you heard a seal bark!" And there was the seal, right above them, you see. And when that was printed, in January 1932, I got a telegram from Bob Benchley. There was nobody whose opinion any American humorist or cartoonist would rather have had, and he said: "Thank you for the funniest drawing caption ever to appear in any magazine!" And when Ross saw that, I became over his dead body an established New Yorker artist.

In the end the wonderful thing was that Ross, who had waved these drawings aside as a gag, and then as a passing fancy of the English—he said that with pleasure and faked gruffness because he loved and admired, as I do, the English—could not get enough of them. Ross just went to any length then to make it possible for my drawings to appear though he had once turned them down. Of course, when he turned my first drawings down and they appeared for the first time in a book, he was beside himself. Here was something creative in his own office, something he'd had first shot at, and it had got into the hands of a publisher who published them—and Ross considered publishers a kind of freak. He didn't think they had any intelligence or any sense . . . Then, of course, he kept at me to send him more drawings and finally I did. But I made him wait a year before I turned them in. Then he found out that I had done 307 drawings for *The New Yorker* with captions, 175 of which had appeared in books.

When I began to go blind it finally got so that I couldn't draw even with black grease crayon on sheets of yellow paper 5 by 4—they had to deal with them like blankets at one time—then I got so I couldn't draw at all, so Ross went through all kinds of worry and suffering about that and said: You see, we can arrange all of it. He decided we would reverse cuts and use new captions; we would cut the drawings up and make permutations. He rearranged the figures of men and women, dogs, furniture, bridge, lamps, and so on . . . And he'd send me captions himself. We did that for a while, but it seemed to me it was a fake. The first publication to notice it—they were not opposed to it, they just said they detected some of my old drawings with new captions—was the *News Chronicle* of London, England.

Finally I said: Well, if we use captions that you or somebody else devises on drawings that I didn't rearrange, I would have no creative part in it. And then I said: You mustn't think I grieve about not being able to draw. If I couldn't write, I couldn't live, but drawing to me was a little bit more than tossing cards in a hat. I think he needed more cheering up about my blindness than I did, you see. That was Ross. That's why it's so wonderful to write about him because he was such a contradictory personality. I imagine Ross now in heaven pacing the Chalcedonian Halls—complaining to some uninterested angel: "What the hell's the matter with the English? Thurber's drawings are not a passing fancy or a fad—they're here to stay. Don't they know that?" Wonderful man to work with . . .

Brandon: Did you develop those characters just by chance—inspiration?

Thurber: Yes. They have been called "unconscious drawings"—a great many of them were unconscious—just start drawing, and suddenly you have it. All the best ones started that way with nothing special in mind. And then I would go from the drawing into the caption. If I started with the caption and then drew the picture to fit it, a stiffness was likely to get into the figures, you see. And then the fact that I was not a draftsman—never took a lesson—can't really draw—

came out. But if the drawings have any merit, it was that they were—some of them—funny. And that's what they were intended to be. They weren't intended to be a special form of art over which I struggled. Because I don't think any drawing ever took me more than three minutes.

I remember when *Life* magazine sent a man over to interview me, and they had devised a little dial with a hand on it and minutes marked off—ten minutes marked off—and they were going to take pictures of me over the course of ten minutes showing the progress of a drawing, I said: "Well, ten seconds would be better!" And there wasn't a drawing I did for them that day that took more than about a minute and ten seconds.

Brandon: It's a sort of—something in between a drawing and a doodle, really—

Thurber: Yes, it is that. I never use the word "doodle"—it always reminds me of a housewife at the telephone trying to get the grocery and being unable to reach them—but there definitely is a resemblance to that, yes, since the best ones were more or less unconscious.

The one that caused the most trouble at *The New Yorker* was the one I described in this new book [*The Years with Ross*], called "The Lady on the Bookcase." It was a nude on all fours on top of the bookcase and a man is saying to a lady visitor: "That's my first wife up there. This is the present Mrs. Harris." And he points to another lady. Well, that upset Ross. He called me on the phone in the country and said: "Is the woman on the bookcase dead or stuffed or alive or what?" And I said: "Well, I'll call you back—I'll have to ask," and hung up. I called him and said: "My doctor says a dead woman couldn't support herself on all fours, and my taxidermist said that you can't stuff a woman—so she must be alive." And Ross roared into the phone: "Then what's she doing in the house of her former husband with his wife—naked?" And I said: "You have me there, Ross, I'm not responsible for the behavior of my characters." But he printed it anyway.

Later I explained to him that I had tried to draw a wife at the head of the stairs—at the head of a flight of stairs waiting for her husband. Having no skill in draftsmanship, I lost perspective and the stairs turned instantly into a bookcase, or what looked like a bookcase, if you made transverse lines—so I made it into a bookcase—and there was this naked lady on top of a bookcase. A great many of the drawings came out accidentally like that—a great many. And it was a great deal of fun not to know what you were going to end up with.

Then, there was the famous incident of Carl Rose's drawing in 1932—very graphic it was, too—of a fencer cutting off his opponent's head and yelling: "Touche!" and the head flies up in the air. Ross thought the Rose drawing—of course, Rose is a fine draftsman and realist—was too bloody and too gruesome. "Let Thurber do it," he said. "Thurber's people don't have blood—you can put their heads right back on, they're as good as new." So I did the drawing and it was run that way and nobody was horrified. But Paul Nash said: "I agree with Ross completely, that this man isn't dead—his head is just off—come off—he's lost his head for the moment."

Nash was extremely anxious to meet Ross. I took him in to see Ross in 1931. I had briefed Ross a little: "You're going to meet a man named Paul Nash—you know nothing about painting—Nash is a distinguished English painter and art critic." Ross said: "Bring him in." So I did. Ross said: "Hi Nash!" That's the way it began—they shook hands—he said again: "Hi Nash!—they're only two phony arts, painting and music." Nash was delighted. Later, he said: "You know, he's like your skyscrapers—they're unbelievable, but there they are." Well, he had a wonderful time.

Brandon: Considering that you illustrate so much the War of the Sexes, your women particularly, have not much sex or sex appeal.

Thurber: It was Marc Connelly who said: "Well, they have for Thurber's men"—when that question was once brought up. But, I should say there were times when I wanted, really, to get a pretty woman in a drawing, and I had toyed with the idea of having some other artist do it. Then I'd draw the rest of the drawing around it, but Ross didn't go for that one. I mean, a luscious Arno girl, for instance . . . with one of my women.

I haven't sent any captions to *The New Yorker* for years. The last one was illustrated by Whitney Darrow. It showed an ardent young lady talking to a gloomy, intellectual young man and she is saying: "When you say you hate your own species, do you mean everybody?" I think that's the last caption of mine they took.

Once I wanted this Dumb Blonde, as we say in America, sitting in

a bar, with a gentleman saying to her: "You complicated little mechanism, you." It seems to me that could be easily done, but . . . again,
that was the kind of thing that frightened Ross. He instantly thought
of physical or even sexual mechanism, you see. His mind—he was
the cleanest-minded man in the world.

He never told a dirty story among men in his life, and he wanted
to keep the magazine clean. He *never* went in once in his life for the
appeal of sensationalism, or sex stuff. In one case, a series of Arno
drawings of a man and a woman supposedly in a compromising
situation on a porch swing—the caption was passionless, such as:
"Have you read any good books lately?" This still appalled Ross so
he made Arno redraw it. Finally I said that the way we ran the series,
the man and woman were approximately as sexually involved as the
husband and his sister-in-law at a christening. But that was Ross, you
see, getting everything as good as possible.

He was afraid of what he called the "functional"—I called him Old-
Chief-Afraid-Of-The-Functional. Once Ross brought to me an Arno
drawing. It showed one of Arno's distinguished Southern gentlemen
of the old school and definitely in his late fifties, dancing with an
ardent young woman and saying: "Good God, woman, think of the
social structure." Well, that threw Ross—he was afraid of the expression "social structure." "Why, in the name of goodness?" I asked.
And he said: "Well, you know, social diseases mean sexual diseases."
And I said: "Dismiss it from your mind, Ross." He just questioned
everything, you see. He was also afraid that some of *The New Yorker*
wits would get things in the magazine that definitely do belong
elsewhere.

Brandon: This idea of a War of Sexes, was that inspired by your
mother? From the description that I've heard of her . . .

Thurber: No, my mother was a great person. I owe practically
everything to her because she was one of the finest comic talents I
think I've ever known—she really was marvelous—she died two
years ago within three weeks of ninety years. And up into her late
eighties she was still comic and played tricks on the telephone with
her friends.

No, I think it's really from having lived two years 1918 and part of
'20 in France—and comparing the life of the French, English, and
other foreigners . . . with family life in America. I could see clearly the

domination of the American woman over her man as compared with that of other countries. America is a matriarchy. It always has been, it always will be. It became obvious to me from the time I was a little boy that the American woman was in charge. I didn't really definitely plan to set out to do that War—I just drew on my unconscious, I guess, and my store of observations about that. I think it's one of the weaknesses of America, the great dominance of the American woman. Not because of that fact in itself, but because she is, as a Chinese woman of distinction said to me some twenty years ago, the least interested in national and international affairs and the most ignorant.

Brandon: But there's a lot of talk about the woman's vote nowadays and its influence . . .

Thurber: Yes, of course, there are so many more women than there are men. The League of Women Voters, the last I heard, had only 127,000 members out of 88 million women in this country and it's very hard for them to get members—women care about other things.

Brandon: But what is different about the American woman, really, from say—

Thurber: I think that Philip Wylie invented the word "Momism." I think that word is a very important word—the mother dominates the son—and every time, I know when he gets home from school in the summertime or wintertime he slams the screen door and says: "Hey—Mom! Can I do this—can I do that?" Permission from "Mom" is the big thing.

Brandon: I presume you mean that there won't be any revolt by American man against the matriarchy—

Thurber: I don't think there will be. Of course, in the series I did, *The War between Men and Women,* the woman surrenders to the man, but you'll notice in the drawings that each woman has a big rock or club behind her back. In other words, the war is not over, so far as she's concerned.

Brandon: But, take Washington, for instance; I can't think of a single woman who plays an important political role behind the scenes, like a Madame Pompadour or—

Thurber: No. No—that brings us back to their weakness in interest in politics, economy, in national affairs. I was very much struck by the fact that the average American woman I know hated history in college. They just don't like history; they know nothing about it, either. So I said that the average American woman, when the war broke out, thought that Pearl Harbor was a movie actress. A young man who works in radio was discussing with me and others one day the average woman and one man said: "What do you mean by the 'average woman'? What do you mean, for instance, by the 'average American woman'—who is she?" And he said: "That's easy. The average American woman wishes her husband was dead and she was in the movies." Well, that's carrying it a little far.

Brandon: I once asked a girl, a married woman in Moscow—where you have so-called equality among the sexes—how she liked that? And she said she'd rather give up her equality . . .

Thurber: You mean she'd rather be the second sex, as the girl in France called it who wrote the book The Second Sex. I do sometimes wish they would.

By the way, the most heartening thing to me that has happened in America for a long time is the Russians getting ahead of us in the Sputniks, because for the first time since the dark ages of McCarthy, the Americans are coming to the realization that God likes other countries as well as this one; that it is possible for American superiority to be exceeded, but once we have to buckle down, we buckle down. I think that has been a very fine thing.

The six or eight years that went by—those terrible years—when all the American Congress seemed to do was to investigate writers, artists, and painters—to me were the dreadful years. All this time Russia was getting ahead of us; all this time we were fighting a new cold civil war—suspecting neighbors, suspecting the very nature of writing, of academic intellectualism, anything—that was a very bad moment in our history—perhaps the darkest we've ever had. But I think we're out of that.

We've always had a belief in push-button superiority and instant lovability—everybody must love us; why shouldn't they, we're Americans! During the darkest years of the McCarthy period, while many writers seemed to be frightened, possibly because they had belonged to some organization when they were in college, they were afraid to write. But I wrote four or five outspoken pieces, because I thought our culture had descended to a pretty low place. Now, when we took the passport away from Arthur Miller—one of the most ridiculous things we ever did, and also one that certainly didn't help our prestige among our allies—I came out, and several of us did, and spoke against that in the New York *Times*. A Congressman had asked him on the stand: 'Do you really believe that the artist is a special person?' Then I wrote in the *Times:* "A nation in which a Congressman can seriously ask: 'Do you think the artist is a special person?' is a nation living in cultural jeopardy." Well, now I think we get farther and farther out of the dark shadows of that cultural jeopardy—and it's a darned good thing.

Americans pride themselves on being a nation of humorists, but I'm afraid that our sense of humor and comedy—certainly sense of humor—does not go very deep. America is the country of the gag, the hot foot, the pay-off, the belly laugh—and that kind of thing. But a basically, imaginative humorous country could never have over-emphasized the way we have overemphasized "Americanism."

I once wrote a small piece about our constant use of "Un-American" when we really mean "patriotic." As if patriotism was a monopoly of the Americans. We would be annoyed and frightened if every time we picked up a foreign paper, there were references to "Englishism"—"Welshism"—"Francism"—"Un-French"—"Un-Belgian."

I have written a little scene in a bar . . . the husband and his wife get into an argument with a man with an accent, and the husband says: "You must be un-American." He says: "I'm a citizen of Oslo." "Then he's un-Swiss," the wife says. "No, I think he's un-Danish." The man finally says: "No, I'm just Norwegian." Well, I wrote that about 1951 and there wasn't anybody who wanted to print that, because we did have the jitters.

Yet, despite the pieces I wrote, nobody ever knocked on my door. Somebody asked a Congressman once—I don't know the Congressman but he's from my state—at a party: "Why have you never investigated Thurber?" And he said—and this is my proudest medal: "Because our wives and daughters wouldn't allow it." I think that's wonderful.

Brandon: It all means, I suppose, that Americans lack the faculty to laugh at themselves.

Thurber: Yes, they think they can, but they really can't. An old professor of mine at college, Professor Joe Taylor said: "A thing that

cannot endure laughter is not a good thing." There was a period—I
wrote about this in some of my pieces—in which we were distinguished for our ability to laugh about ourselves, the days of
Mencken, Will Rogers, William Allen White, and many others, with
either a broad sword or a slapstick, you know, making fun of Congressman. But then we got scared of 'em. And that's a bad thing
when we get scared of our Congressman, because a lot of them are
buffoons. When you get right down to it, we're only scared to death
in peacetimes—we're wonderful warriors, you know—but it's the
jitteriest country in peacetimes.

Put your head out the window and yell: *Here it comes!*—and
everybody rushes out on the street. There was actually, some years
ago during the dark ages of the McCarthy period, a tremendous
hailstorm in Martha's Vineyard—half the size of golf balls—the hail
fell on the ancient town of Edgartown which was founded during the
reign of King James the First . . . I think—named after his oldest
son—I may have the kings wrong . . . but they thought: Here comes
the bombs—they're now the size of golf balls. Something new. And
everybody ran out on the streets and got slugged on the head with
these things, in spite of the orders from civilian security to stay in-
doors. Our desire to take to the open is a panic urge. We're living on
the edge of the abyss. As somebody said, the fascination of the edge
of the abyss. But I'm very hopeful that America has finally seen that
it's got to buckle down and get to work.

Our strength is our weakness and it may get so that we mistake
loose talk for free speech and the freedom of liberty for complacency—you see, we don't have to do anything, everything's going to be
fine because this is God's country. I did one caption for *The New
Yorker* which was printed some years ago. It showed a meeting of
representatives of all the nations of the world—just at the opening of
the United Nations—and an American saying: "It's a wonderful thing
to co-operate with all our friends and allies right here in God's
country."

You see, we can't get it out of our minds that this is where God
lives—He never even visits any place else. If, as I say, we were a
nation of humorists, as we think we are, we would appreciate these
things. Actually, during the jitteriest period *The Male Animal*—a play
that I wrote with Elliott Nugent in 1940—it ran eight months—was

revived in 1952 and ran ten months. It was put on by a company in a small town in California, Laguna Beach. The review was headlined: "Americans attacked at Playhouse!" Well, I had some real fun with that one. I actually laughed him out of existence. I said: "Well, don't you realize I intended to undermine America in three acts. I also undermined American womanhood, and wives and football players and everything else—and they ought to come and get me for it." And I said: "After all, when people went to see that play, they joined the party fast—either the Democrats or the Republicans or the one going on to Twenty-One after the play." And then I said: "I might as well confess the whole thing—now that they're on to me as an underminer—*The New Yorker* really got its name so that we could chang the 'Y' to 'W' overnight and become *The New Worker*." Well, it turned out the country could—and did—take that as a kind of ridicule of the intimidation and oppression, and it was high time somebody was doing it. I got no bad reactions from it whatever and I got a great many letters from all over the country praising our play. Rather sheepishly the Laguna Beach paper printed an editorial as if *The Male Animal* were an attack on the United States of America . . . Well, it does mention Abraham Lincoln's name in the same breath with Sacco and Vanzetti. My heavens, I also mentioned Herbert Hoover's name in the same breath . . . Of all the people who ever lived, the one who would most have approved of that was one Abraham Lincoln, you know. "If you have enough breath," he once said, "you can mention anybody's name with mine."

Brandon: In this present generation there are few, if any, humorists, really.

Thurber: It is a curious thing . . . I did some research on that. In the 1920s when Ross said that humorists were a dime a dozen, they practically were. Sally Benson appeared in 1929 and then in 1930, Ogden Nash and S. J. Perelman; after that the pickings have been very few. We've had Peter de Vries, in the last twelve or fourteen years, and John McNulty. But the young people are not funny . . .

I found out in addressing college classes—journalism classes years ago—that since the mental weather of the 1920s there's been a definite decline into grimness. They used to ask me: How old is Peter Arno? What is Dorothy Parker like? And now they ask me what I believe about the future of America—or what is my artistic credo?

Everybody is getting very serious. You can just sense that change; the
beginning of a kind of a chill.

It is very hard to sustain humor—the desire for humor—in a period
when mankind seems to be trying, on the one hand, to invent a pill
or miracle drug that will cure us all of everything; with the other hand,
it's inventing a machine for instant annihilation—you just light the
fuse and Bang! Up go all the healthy people. Now that, of course, is
part of the dichotomy of the very nature of our species, which makes
it interesting and also terrifying.

If there is life on other planets, they must be scared to death of us,
sending things up that may finally bring one man of another race to
their planet. That would scare me if I lived on Venus, where they
must be having a lovely time, if it's anything like its name.

Brandon: Pity Venus is not within rocket-shot. It sounds much
more enticing than the moon. Talking about gadgets, and I mean
entirely earthbound ones, an incident comes to my mind which, I
think, is perfect Thurberism. It happened at an embassy in Washington the other day. The ambassador or minister or whoever it was had
the usual two telephones on his desk, but both suddenly seemed out
of order. When the telephone rang and he lifted the receiver, he
didn't hear anything and when he lifted the receiver to make a call
the second telephone sounded dead. The mechanic came, but he
could not find anything wrong with the telephones; it looked like a
mischievous mystery until he found that the receivers had been on
the wrong telephones. (*Laughter*)

Thurber: Wonderful.

Brandon: It's as universal as Thurberism. Talking about universal
humor—do you understand the humor in *Punch?*

Thurber: I haven't had a chance to see *Punch,* really, I've been so
busy just writing about *The New Yorker,* but actually—here I go with
my English "actually"—to read *The New Yorker*   takes a lot of time.
Johnny Miller—John Duncan Miller, the former *Times* of London
man in Washington—said to me once: "I used to be able to read *The
New Yorker* coming up from Washington to New York. Now if you
want to finish it, you have to go at least as far as San Diego." Some
3000 miles . . . We have got into a thing that Ross dreaded all his
life—the magazine is turning grim and long. In the early days, he
used to pay a premium for stories under 2000 words and even more

word-rate if it was under 1000. If you ran past 5000 it was as little as three cents a word extra, you see, which is a valiant but 'fewtle'—'futile' gesture.

Brandon: In your earlier days at *The New Yorker* writers with new ideas probably had a much better chance to get a hearing. Now *The New Yorker* has its style—its tradition—its format, and everybody tries to conform to that . . .

Thurber: Yes, yes . . . that's one of the troubles that a magazine is likely to settle into a kind of formula. It's hard . . . It's now a great big business over there—writing and editing—it's terrific. All of us worry about its increase in size, wealth and what I call "matronly girth"—but it lacks comedy. It's very hard to break into *The New Yorker*. They're not really looking for humor—they don't expect it, so they don't really encourage humor. As I said in one piece, Ross used to say: "We're in a velvet rut"—by which I think he meant the stuff is pretty average, but we're making money out of it.

But now we're in a tulle and taffeta rut, 'cause everybody's writing about—and this seems to me a curious escapism—their girlhood, young womanhood, first baby, first year of marriage, and so on. Then *The New Yorker* uses so many women on an island—well, that's a form of escape, too, I think. And then our great love of Westerns—the President reads Westerns—and television is almost dominated by Westerns, you know. Yet if you see those Westerns, they're bloody and cruel and certainly no escape in that sense. *My Fair Lady* was written before the First World War—that is, the Shaw play. There is a return to the past, you see, as a form of escape. It's impossible to analyze it off-hand, but I do feel that people are trying to get away from the terrible pressure of man as a purely political and cold war creature. The strain is terrific.

Brandon: Also there isn't enough irreverence—there is no magazine or no newspaper, really, where irreverence can find an entry.

Thurber: That's right. You mean as in the day, for instance, of Henry Mencken's *American Mercury*. Yes, we have nothing like that, that's true. There again, the craziness of the 1920s was counterbalanced by its great sense of freedom and liberty of expression—take John Dos Passos' *Three Soldiers*. You could write about anything and nobody was afraid of anybody. Americans were not afraid of Americans. That's the thing that frightens me about America is our tendency to carry on the Civil War in some way.

We've always had this tremendously competitive spirit among Americans, you see. Yesterday, not content with having a football season of professional football, we ended up with a "Bowl" Game in which you select men from the East and the West and then you have them go at each other. And the day before, we had the North and the South—fighting each other in football—in amateur football. In some ways that's healthy, and in some ways it isn't.

Brandon: How do you feel about the state of American writing?

Thurber: I think it was Edmund Wilson who said that at his age— he's a year younger than I—"You really haven't got time left to spend on contemporary writers because you wouldn't get anything else done." The tendency of a person in his sixties is to go back and read the classics and the great books that you have been putting aside, saying: "I'll take that one with me to Bermuda"—you know—they pile up and you don't get around. So I'm really not competent to judge.

I do have a definite sense that humor and comedy are declining. It shows up in the New York theater. The tendency is to turn to farce rather than high comedy. I was very much impressed when I saw *The Chalk Garden* because that came like a fresh breeze of comedy out of England. I wrote that you felt the girl who wrote this play was writing in a truly free atmosphere, unafraid of criticism or intimidation or of anything else. And it shows up in the ease of writing. Very often the English or foreign play has an effect that we don't have. We seem to have lost respect for comedy in this country. Comedy has declined tremendously on television—to an astonishing and disheartening degree. People get the idea that comedy is easy—comedy is very hard to do right. It is a very important thing, too, and there are not very many holding on. For instance, Sid Perelman [S. J.] still writes a lot—and I still get quite a deal written, but Andy White [E. B.] and Frank Sullivan don't do very much any more. But there may be, I hope there will be, a renaissance of comedy—good comedy—for the very fact that *My Fair Lady* exhilarated this country beyond belief. There's no parallel. We've finally got back to high comedy—and everybody loved it.

Brandon: Do you prefer human beings or animals, really?

Thurber: I have my moods. Often I think it would be fine if the French poodle could take over the world because they've certainly been more intelligent in the last few years than the human being, and they have great charm, grace, humor, and intelligence. My old poodle, who died at seventeen, had genuine comic sense . . . But, as I say, when I spoke to the poodle about her species taking over, she said: "The hell with it!" They don't want to get mixed up in it.

But what troubles me most about today are our children. In his recent State of the Union speech two things amused and depressed me that the President said. One was his romantic appeal to the "schoolboy with his bag of books and his homework." Our schoolboys, I am afraid, lack mental discipline. We have a frightened inability to appreciate discipline. We instantly call it, even essential mental discipline, "regimentation," and dismiss it as Communistic. We confuse it with political regimentation. Our kids have given up hard work. Every year, for instance, I get hundreds of letters from English language students from all parts of he United States asking me for biographical material.

Some teachers started a few years ago in what we call junior high school the idea of assigning English classes to write about a given writer—and they said: "Why don't you write to him and ask him a few intelligent questions?" Well, from all over the country came letters . . . Steinbeck was so overwhelmed with letters that he wrote a piece of protest about it in the *Saturday Review of Literature* saying they get peremptory, don't send any. We all had to get up a form letter telling some facts about ourselves. But they don't want that.

I sat down and wrote one boy the other day, named Robert—and their letters are so illiterate and badly spelled—he said: "My English clarr . . . "—this was how he typed it out—and I said: "How in the world could you do that when the 's' follows the 'a' on the keyboards and the 'r' is on the line above?" And I continued: "You live in New York City—I occasionally help out kids who write me from the small towns, where there's no library available—but you can find out in one afternoon all the 'biographical material' as you call it, about me." He wrote back and said: "If you don't send me some biographical material I'll write to another writer." They don't want biographical material; they want us to do their homework. In one case I wrote back that I spent two years studying the facts about the Loch Ness monster before doing my story about it, but that I never wrote to it.

The other thing that amused and depressed me about the President's speech was his use of the word "finalize." My most intense dedication now is the defense of the English language against the decline it has suffered in this century and particularly since the end of the last war.

My country has always cared little for exactness in language and has always depreciated good English as "book larnin." Those of us who are dedicated to good English as the very basis of communication and understanding have been called everything from Teacher's pet to egghead and nobody is more to blame than members of Congress. They should be regularly punished by fine and one day's confinement in the third grade of grammar school.

In one of the pieces of my book *Alarms and Diversions* called "The Psychosemanticist Will See You Now, Mr. Thurber," there's a complaint about what I call "Congressionalese." It ends up with the story that under President Eisenhower some bureau in Washington sent out to all other bureaus a letter to protest against the use of certain fake words like "finalize." So what does the President do but use "finalize" in his State of the Union address. That awful, fake, synthetic word . . . but now he's finalized "finalize"—so we'll never get rid of finalize. His diction too is careless. He says individual as if it was spelled "individjel." Wendell Wilkie too said: "The 'Nine States of America" and "the great resarvar of foreign friendship for us." The very basis of human communication and understanding is language. And when I turn on the radio and listen to discussions at the United Nations, the English representatives speak beautiful English and so do the foreigners, from the Orient, from anywhere. Their English is excellent. The American is likely to be sloppy and full of slang.

I was very much impressed by reading the English papers to see how carefully they write criticism of the theater or books—or of anything else. It's done with loving and painstaking care and we just seem to have thrown English to the wolves. We don't care what we say or how we say it. I'm afraid I'm waging a losing battle trying to do anything about it. I was very pleased to print something by—I can't recall his name right now, an Englishman who told exactly how

Americans would say Winston Churchill's great line: "Give us the
tools and we will finish the job." "Supply us with the instruments and
we will finalize the undertaking." That's *pure* American—pure Congressionalese. If we went out into the streets dressed the way we talk,
we would be arrested for indecent exposure.

My basic worry has been the necessity of our understanding each
other. For instance, in London I met a girl who, at that time, had lived
and worked in New York for nine years. We got to discussing the
English language, about which I had written a great many pieces.
And when I asked her what word—what American pronunciation
annoyed her most, she said: "The way you say 'fewtle' for 'futile.' "
And I said: "Well, I'll come back at you, you're right. 'Futile' is a
lovely word—the 'ile' is like a chord on a mandolin and must be
sounded. If we spelled our word out the way *we* pronounce it, it
would be 'fewtle.' But you people ruin a lovely piano chord when
you change 'figure' to 'figger'—so we come out even."

There's another interesting thing—since I have this profound
interest in words and speech . . . When I was in England twenty
years ago, people were saying "actually"—when they don't always
mean it, and also "as a matter of fact." But I was terribly impressed
the last time with the fact that almost all Englishmen now use a gesture of speech which has a curious sound—and I started a piece
about it called "The Very Best Butter" for *Punch* when Mr. Muggeridge was still editor—I'd even hear it on the BBC: "Oh yes, I was
there but-ta that was years ago . . . " and then you'd get the real
triple effect: "Yes, I've been in India, its true but-tmm-ah . . . " you
see, then you give it the three sound—and I noticed it in practically
anybody. You haven't got it, but I notice it in almost everybody I'd
see.

It's a little gesture as of lighting a cigarette or sipping from a glass
while they think of the next phrase, you see. Ours, of course, is "and-
da"—and that's . . an American woman's "and-da" comes when
she can't actually think what she's going to say and has lost track.
She'll say: "So we went to this party and-da—and-da . . . " But the
English don't lose track of what they're saying, they just put that
lovely coupling as between two cars in a railroad train—"But-tmm—
and it fascinates me. When the English say the King's English—now
the Queen's English, I suppose—they really mean something by that.

Harold Ross used to give to each one of us, when we started to work there, a copy of Fowler's *Modern English Usage.* He knew it by heart—it's a wonderful book. I did a parody of it called *Our Own Modern English Usage* and got a very nice letter from Fowler's secretary—this was way back, thirty years ago. I gave Ross an earlier book that Fowler had done called *The King's English.* But, you see, that's a term of vast respect for language—the King's English—we don't have that. Save us from the President's English!

Brandon: I feel that I have complete contact with you. Can you see me?

Thurber: No, I can't see a thing—

Brandon: But I have a feeling that you can see me, really—

Thurber: I know, I fool people. I have actually sat all evening with people and they didn't realize that I couldn't see them—at least, dimly—but that's just what the doctors call "accommodation."

See, I started to go slowly blind in 1940—I lost my left eye in an accident when I was only six; with glasses I could see very well until I was forty-five and then the cataract set in and complications—so that I have every known disease from glaucoma to grade A iritis and a thing called "sympathetic ophthalmia." But what happened was that the sight, which I still have and can't get at, is covered by what they call "the thickening of the capsule" from which they take the cataract. I now live in a soft diffusion of light—and it's very pleasant, it's very soft—it's a light without landscape or figures, you see, just a definite diffusion of light.

But I look at voices—people talking—turn my head—because I was always appalled at the blind man who doesn't look at anybody . . . but that's a sheer matter of accommodation. The process started in 1940, very gradually, so that I almost was unaware of it and then it got so I couldn't see.

In 1951, a man who was almost blind, an Englishman living in Manchester, England, sent me what he called a luminous white crayon and dead black paper—all of it by airmail. And with that I could really do some of my last drawings because the white line on the black paper gleamed.

Another thing that is very moving and I like to tell—I don't know if it embarrasses Helen. When she and I both had eye trouble—she was in the hospital with a detached retina—I got letters from ten strangers, two from England, offering to give an eye. They were people with perfect sight, offering to give me or Helen one of their eyes. One of them came from an English gardener in Sussex. He said: "I am thirty-four, married, I have two daughters, seven and four, I have very strong eyes, I am willing to give you one because of the pleasure I've got out of your books."

Well, I had to write to all these ten people saying this: "Since the human being is so ignorant about the eye, the only thing that can be transplanted is the cornea. The cornea is that transparent covering of the whole eyeball, you can get that. But you cannot transplant anything else. Furthermore, no doctor in the world, no ophthalmologist or eye surgeon, would perform what they call a prophylactic operation on a good eye, for the simple reason that they do not know what effect that would have on the other one." But for ten people—strangers to me—to be willing to give up one of their eyes, isn't that wonderful? That's the kind of thing that doesn't get in the papers about human beings, isn't it? We hear all about the ones that gouge eyes out—but we don't hear about the ones who offer their good eyes.

Brandon: Once I interviewed Axel Munthe, who then was blind. I had the strange experience that when I entered his house, he put both of his hands on my face and he said: "You have a good face— come in."

Thurber: I never tried the sense of touch on friends like that—to see how accurate it would be . . . But it is amazing how you depend more on your ear. For instance, at a party at my house a few years ago, a big party, I said later—after a certain couple had left— "They're going to break up." And they all thought I'd lost my mind. They said: "Why, we have never seen such friendliness and smiling." I said: "Yes, you looked at them—I heard them." And they lasted six months after that.

There's something about voice that is destroyed if you are watching the expression of the face. It will mislead you sometimes. Everybody looks at the eyes and expression, but I concentrate on inflection, intonation, and dropping and raising of the voice—and often surprise people by saying: "What's happened?"—"Well, how do you know that sort of thing?"—"Well, I can tell . . . " Although they're saying something that isn't sorrowful or serious or tragic, you can tell.

A man asked me if I could get my sight back for one day, who would I want to see? Marilyn Monroe? I said: "No, I want to see some old friends of mine. I have a pretty good idea what Marilyn Miller must look like—"

Brandon: Have you heard the definition of an "egghead"? Someone who calls Marilyn Monroe "Mrs. Arthur Miller."

Thurber: That's very good. Phillip Halsman, the photographer, told me how difficult it was to get different expressions on her face, yet she's a great comic. To get a special new look on her face he said to her: "How old were you when you had your first affair with a man?" And she said: "Seven"—she knew exactly what he was up to—and didn't change at all. When the same photographer was talking to me, he led me over to a chair, an ordinary kitchen chair, cheap, wooden chair, and he said: "Lean back on this." I said: "What shall I lean against?" He said: "Against this old-fashioned brick fireplace I've had put in here—nineteenth-century America." And I said: "What's the idea?" "Because I feel you're rugged." I said: "Oh boy, you've found the word that appeals to most American men, but I'm not 'rugged'." Every American, I guess, would love to be thought of as an Abe Lincoln leaning back against the fireplace. That's the old self-made, rugged American type . . . The other type is "Outdoors Western," or "Silent Jim." Helen says I'll never be called "Silent Jim."

Brandon: I sometimes get the impression from your writings that you really would have preferred to live in a different century.

Thurber: Henry James' great desire, and I don't share this with him, was to have lived in what he called the "Baronic Period"—the English 1820s, around there . . . Of course, I've been considered a great Henry James man and I do admire him as a craftsman very much. But the more I reread Henry James, the more I realize he didn't have a great deal to say except in skill and in the relationships of sensibilities—rather than the clash of anything more important.

My love of London and of England is inherited from somewhere, although my family on both sides have been over here since the eighteenth century. I still feel a sense of "getting home" when I get to London, to England. It is a country where you can hear bells ring. By the way, when we were in London in 1955, we called—as we always do when we're there—on John Hayward who, at that time, was sharing an apartment in Cheney Walk with T. S. Eliot. And Eliot said, pointing to the ceiling above: "I don't want you to think I moved in here for this reason, but I just found out the other day that Henry James died in that room above here."

And he asked me if I knew what his last words were supposed to have been. I said, "No, I hadn't heard that." And he said: "He was supposed to have said: 'The inevitable end—the distinguished thing'." Well I've been thinking about that for two years and while "the inevitable end" anybody might say, "the distinguished thing" sounds exactly like a Henry James title for a short story, such as "The Great Good Place," "The Distinguished Thing," "The Stronger Sense," or anything . . . But I think that his voice was getting low and that what he really said was "the extinguished flame."

I do not believe that Henry James would consider distinguished something that happens to everybody. I want to see what his reaction to that would be.

But I'm satisfied living in this century. If you lived in any other century, you would miss some of the greatest and most appalling things . . . Well, to use the phrase of the greatest phrasemaker of our time, Sir Winston Churchill: "The awful and the magnificent." He was speaking of the A-bomb—that awful and magnificent weapon. Well, this is an awful and magnificent century to live in, and I wouldn't miss that.

Index

Harris, Frank, 59
Hawthorne, Nathaniel, 59
Hayward, John, 115–16
Hemingway, Ernest, 16, 46, 60, 62–63
Hergesheimer, Joseph, 60, 63; *Wild Oranges,*
   60
Hitler, Adolf, 62
Hobson, Laura, 46
Holiday, 36
Hoover, Herbert, 106
Housman, Laurence, 44

I

Irvin, Rea, 96

J

James, Henry, 29, 54, 58–59, 77, 115–16
Johnson, Nunnally, 46
Johnson, Spud, 38
Joyce, James, *Finnegan's Wake,* 36

K

Kafka, Franz, *The Castle,* 36; *The Trial,* 36
Kanode, Bob, 72
Keats, John, 63
Kenyon College, 20, 73
Khrushchev, Mrs. Nikita, 89
Khrushchev, Nikita, 89
Killiam, Bert, 21–22
Klein, Norman, *No, No, the Woman,* 46
Kober, Arthur, 38
Kuchner, Norman, "Gus," 73

L

Liberty and Justice Book Award, 41
Life, 36, 70, 99
Lincoln, Abraham, 106
Lincoln, Victoria, *February Hill,* 60
Loch Ness monster, 43
Lost Lady, A (Cather), 59

M

Maloney, Russell, 15
Marx, Groucho, 69
Matisse, Henri, 96
McCarthyism, 66, 76, 78, 103–5
McNulty, John, 106
Mead, Margaret, 77

Mencken, H. L., 31, 47, 59, 105, 108;
   American Mercury, 108
Miller, Arthur, 103–4, 115
Miller, John Duncan, 107
"Momism," 102
Monroe, Marilyn, 115
Mt. Holyoke College, 84
Muggeridge, Malcolm, 111
Munthe, Axel, 114
Museum of Modern Art, 5

N

Nash, Ogden, 7, 16, 38, 106
Nash, Paul, 95, 100
New Statesman, The, 96
New York Herald Tribune, 45
New York Post, The, 16–17, 20, 46, 71
New York Times, The, 57, 104
New Yorker, The, 3, 4, 6, 10–11, 19, 20,
   28–29, 30, 36–37, 39, 43, 45–46, 48,
   49–50, 57–58, 60, 62, 65–66, 70,
   71–72, 80, 82, 94–96, 98–101, 105–8
News Chronicle, The, 98
Night and Day, 96
Nixon, Richard, 78
Nugent, Elliott, 3–4, 7–8, 12, 21, 30–31, 44,
   54, 72–73, 105–6

O

O'Hara, John, 62–63
Ohio State Journal, The, 17
Ohio State University, 3, 19–22, 27, 38, 43,
   47, 70, 72–73, 82, 90
Oxford English Dictionary, 65

P

Parker, Dorothy, 38, 53, 62, 65, 106
Paul, Elliot, 55
Perelman, S.J., 38, 106, 109
Pickwick Papers, The (Dickens), 31
Punch, 61, 107, 112

R

Red Badge of Courage, The (Crane), 59
Rogers, Will, 79, 105
Roosevelt, Franklin D., 17–18
Roosevelt, Mrs. Kermit, 17
Rose, Carl, 100
Rose, Leroy, 21–22

Lightning Source UK Ltd.
Milton Keynes UK
UKOW04f0054201114

241867UK00026B/506/A